CARVING WOODEN ANIMALS

E.J. Tangerman

STERLING PUBLISHING CO., INC. NEW YORK

About the Author

E. J. Tangerman has been carving for over fifty years and has visited and studied in most of the well-known woodcarving areas around the world. He is currently vice-president of the National Wood Carvers Association.

Mr. Tangerman is the author of a number of woodcarving reference books, including "Whittling and Woodcarving," which has become the basic text in the field. He has written articles for such magazines as *Popular Mechanics* and *Popular Science Monthly*, and is a frequent contributor to *Chip Chats*, the NWCA magazine, and to the *Bulletin of the International Wood Collectors Society*.

Fourth Printing, 1981

Contents

Woodworkers' Conversion Tables

Imperial inches	Metric millimetres	Woodworkers' parlance (mm)
$\frac{1}{32}$	0.8	1
$\frac{1}{16}$	1.6	$1\frac{1}{2}$
$\frac{1}{8}$	3.2	3
$\frac{3}{16}$	4.8	5
$\frac{1}{4}$	6.4	$6\frac{1}{2}$
$\frac{5}{16}$	7.9	8
$\frac{3}{8}$	9.5	$9\frac{1}{2}$
$\frac{7}{16}$	11.1	11
$\frac{1}{2}$	12.7	$12\frac{1}{2}$
$\frac{9}{16}$	14.3	$14\frac{1}{2}$
$\frac{5}{8}$	15.9	16
$\frac{11}{16}$	17.5	$17\frac{1}{2}$
$\frac{3}{4}$	19.1	19
$\frac{13}{16}$	20.6	$20\frac{1}{2}$
$\frac{7}{8}$	22.2	22
$\frac{15}{16}$	23.8	24
1	25.4	$25\frac{1}{2}$
2	50.8	51
3	76.2	76
4	101.4	$101\frac{1}{2}$
5	127.0	127
6	152.4	$152\frac{1}{2}$
7	177.5	$177\frac{1}{2}$
8	203.2	203
9	228.6	$228\frac{1}{2}$
10	254.0	254
11	279.5	$279\frac{1}{2}$
12	304.8	305
18	457.2	457
24	609.6	$609\frac{1}{2}$
36	914.4	$914\frac{1}{2}$

Metric millimetres	Imperial inches	Woodworkers' parlance (mm)
1	0.039	$\frac{1}{16}$
2	0.078	$\frac{1}{16}$
3	0.118	$\frac{1}{8}$
4	0.157	$\frac{5}{32}$
5	0.196	$\frac{3}{16}$
6	0.236	$\frac{1}{4}$
7	0.275	$\frac{1}{4}$
8	0.314	$\frac{5}{16}$
9	0.353	$\frac{3}{8}$
10	0.393	$\frac{3}{8}$
20	0.787	$\frac{13}{16}$
30	1.181	$1\frac{3}{16}$
40	1.574	$1\frac{9}{16}$
50	1.968	$1\frac{15}{16}$
60	2.362	$2\frac{3}{8}$
70	2.755	$2\frac{3}{4}$
80	3.148	$3\frac{1}{8}$
90	3.542	$3\frac{9}{16}$
100	3.936	$3\frac{15}{16}$
150	5.904	$5\frac{15}{16}$
200	7.872	$7\frac{7}{8}$
300	11.808	$11\frac{13}{16}$
400	15.744	$15\frac{3}{4}$
500	19.680	$19\frac{11}{16}$
600	23.616	$23\frac{5}{8}$
700	27.552	$27\frac{9}{16}$
800	31.488	$31\frac{1}{2}$
900	35.424	$35\frac{7}{16}$
1,000	39.360	$39\frac{3}{8}$

Note: The imperial and metric sizes given for tools and joint parts, etc., cannot work out exactly, but providing you work to one or the other there is no difficulty. In the timber trade it is accepted that 1 in = 25 mm.

Before You Carve

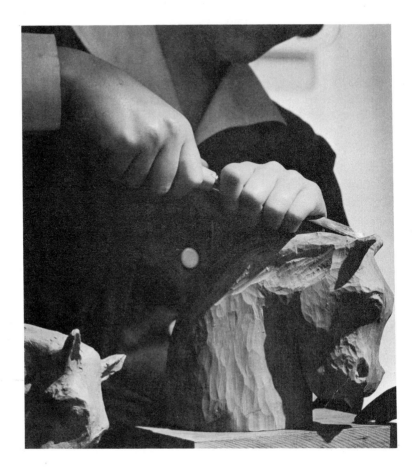

IN PAPEETE, a New York hotel designer sat with a Tahitian woodcarver to negotiate a price for thirty tikis (Polynesian wood images). The first, they agreed, would cost 2,000 Tahitian francs. "And for the next twenty-nine tikis?" asked the designer. "They will be more than 3,000 francs each," the carver said. "But why?" "Because only the first one is fun."

Neil Morgan told the story in *Saturday Review*. Sharing that carver's sentiments, I have spent whatever time I have had available for fifty years, seeking out what for me were new ideas for carvings, simple or complex. I have less interest in the familiar and traditional European patterns but much more in the things that primitive, and often self-taught, carvers make purely for the love of it. Somehow, such carvings are less rigid, less standardized, less florid, and far more imaginative—full of verve and of life. I bought those I could afford and that were for sale, and photographed or sketched others. Retirement has made it possible for me to visit many of the less well known parts of the world where carving is still respected and admired.

In recent years relatively high incomes and early retirement have provided many people with leisure time as well as the wherewithal to do with it what they want. Out of this and an increasing disaffection with prepackaged, all-alike products—which many of us have spent our working lifetimes helping to make—has risen a tremendous craft movement, the desire to do one's own thing. As a result, what was once dismissed as primitive, folk, or naive art is coming to be recognized, because of its strength and originality, as fully comparable with the often slavish and more rigid productions of academic art.

My effort here is to capture not only examples of American folk art but those typical of faraway places, to give you a source for new and different ideas upon which to build. This volume is devoted to subjects quite familiar to most primitive carvers but less familiar to Americans—the world of mammals, birds and fishes, and even a saurian or two. Ancient man respected, feared and admired the inhabitants of that world; the development of cities and highways has tended to take us out of it, even to destroy it, at an accelerating rate.

I have tried to maintain logical groupings of the designs presented here, and yet to grade them so we begin with the simplest and end with the most complex. The first few chapters include carvings that can be made with the knife alone, while most of the remainder can be done with relatively few and inexpensive tools. This grading is based upon my own experience in carving them; indeed, many of my own designs and carvings are scattered through the book. I have provided such patterns as are necessary, and detailed instructions where difficulty might be encountered, plus tips, shortcuts and suggestions. There are also answers to the basic questions of the neophyte, to make this volume complete in itself. I have also included examples of recent original work of other Americans who are more concerned with the enjoyment to be gotten from carving than with possible income from it, and who whittle or carve as an avocation or leisure-time pursuit. They understand the Tahitian carver's reluctance to turn himself into a production machine. If you are also reluctant, this book was written for you.

E. J. TANGERMAN

6

CHAPTER I

Answers to Your Basic Questions

What is whittling? What is woodcarving?

WHITTLE was originally an Old English word for a butcher knife, but now is largely obsolete except in Scotland and in dialect, in which it also means blanket or flannel petticoat. It has no connection with woodcarving except in the United States, where, according to Webster, the verb means "to cut or shape a piece of wood by slowly paring it away with a knife."

Actually, the definition has been more precise than that. Among whittlers it means carving with a clasp knife a *one-piece* object of wood, usually small enough to be held in the hand. However, as might be expected, modern technology has loosened the definition by providing special whittling knives with fixed or interchangeable blades, plus myriad other tools designed to do a particular job or speed the work in general. Even sandpaper might be called a multiple knife because each tiny grain actually scratches away a chip.

The same might be said about woodcarving, which originally was understood to mean the shaping of wood with traditional tools such as firmers, gouges and the adz, with riffler files and rasps thrown in. Modern technology has, however, added such tools as the bandsaw, chain saw, flexible-shaft machines, hand-held grinders, rotary and belt sanders and pneumatic or electric hammers. All sorts of accessories have been added as well, including special-position vises, multiple forms of mallet, stands and worktables of special design. Even in woodcarving, the urge to mechanize has its adherents, particularly among those caught up in the desire to make a profit, either from woodcarvings or selling the increasingly expensive equipment—or even to save time.

All this tends to obscure the fact that woodcarving, like whittling, can be and is being done with very limited numbers of tools—and no other equipment whatsoever. The carver in Bali or Easter Island, in both of which woodcarving is the only industry, rarely has more than four or five tools and probably uses a shaped club for a mallet and his knees for a vise. His tools are usually home-made and cherished, not for their number or variety but for their necessity. His "shop," like the whittler's here, is portable. In fact, only in Europe and America have all the devices for saving time been introduced, and in both places we also have duplicating machines, profilers and plastic-and-sawdust moulded fakes.

What tools do you need to whittle?
(Tool illustrations on pgs. 10–11.)

YOU NEED a good knife, if you can get one. Most modern knives have stainless-steel blades, which don't rust but also don't hold an edge. Better is an old-fashioned pocketknife with carbon-steel blades (A). For conventional whittling, two blades are enough; three may be a help, but more than that tends to increase bulk and weight in the hand. I carry two pocketknives, one regular size with three blades, a pen, a spear, and a B-clip (B); the smaller, a penknife with one pen and a B-clip. Thus I have both small and large blades, wide and narrow, short- or long-pointed.

When I'm at home, I use either a fixed-blade knife, which is safer (a pocket-knife blade, carelessly handled, can close on a finger) and more comfortable to grip because of the larger handle, or two of the modern plastic handles with heavy-duty replaceable blades. One blade is a modified B-clip shape, the other a so-called hook blade designed for leather working. For most work, a blade $1\frac{1}{2}$ in (4 cm) long is plenty. Longer than that it begins to require extra gripping and may catch near the handle on parts of the piece you don't want to cut. The wider the blade, the straighter and more stable the cut, because of the added surface resting on the work. The narrower the blade, the greater the ease of carving in tight places and on concave surfaces, but greater control is needed, and there is greater likelihood of breakage.

The warning to cut away from yourself doesn't work in whittling any more than it does in peeling potatoes. The sketches (pgs. 12–13) show the many ways in which cuts can be made. You'll need them all before you're through, although some are much more important than others. Here are additional pointers:

Chips should be cut out, not wedged out—a hard lesson to learn—and a major reason why the rotary-chuck disposable-blade handles must be kept supertight. The blade may rotate in the handle or snap off. For some detail, a narrow, thin blade may be helpful; sometimes a sharp V-point is essential. Whittlers grind special knives and points for such jobs, using old straight razors, discarded hacksaw blades, even scissors or other pieces of hardened tool steel. I've made special long-handled knives to put a ship in a bottle by breaking off (with a pair of pliers) narrow sections of safety-razor blades and binding them in dowel-rod handles. An endless variety of blade shapes and lengths is possible, of course. You don't need them unless you specialize.

Beware of too-large and too-heavy handles with too-rigid, finger-shaped impressions, blades that are thin or wobble sideways and knives that do not snap open and shut securely. (The Swedes avoid this with the barrel knife, which has one blade that is opened, then thrust—and locked—through the handle. These have a sloyd blade—thick at the heel—which is stiff enough for heavy cutting, but may make trouble on delicate cuts.)

Knives must be kept sharp to reduce the cutting force required, because added force means lessened control and faster tiring, plus torn rather than cut wood fibers. Good steel, properly sharpened and honed, will hold its edge all day in whittling soft wood, but the hard wood will require a touch-up every hour or so. A portable fine-grained stone and a hone (leather glued on a stick and oiled) are essential; to do a clean cutting job in finishing you need a very sharp edge.

A knife can be dangerous, so be careful; never put anything in front of the blade that you don't intend to cut. Initially, you may want to wear a rubber or plastic finger stall on your thumb (stationery shops sell them for people who do counting and sorting) and a Band-Aid, tape, or other insulator on the middle joint of your index finger to prevent blisters. Keep your mind on what you are doing; whittling can be very relaxing, but it isn't like knitting—it isn't something to keep nervous hands busy while you watch TV or converse.

If you stick the tip of the blade into the work, be sure the pressure is in the direction of the cutting edge; a blade closing on a finger is no joke. To close the blade, hold the knife handle carefully in the fingertips and close the blade with the palm of the other hand. Don't open two blades at once. If the blade has no boss, be careful that your finger doesn't slip forward onto the sharp edge. Don't hammer the blade or use it to cut newspaper clippings or fiber tapes or fingernails—or, Lord forbid, scrape insulation from wire. Don't cut newly sanded surfaces. All these destroy the alignment of the tiny tips on the so-called feather edge of the blade, and make it dull (see Sharpening, pgs. 120–124).

9

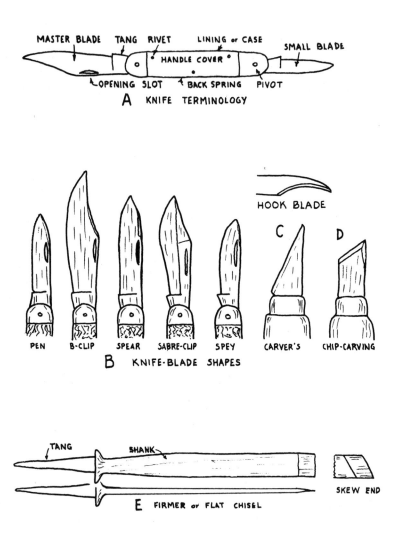

MASTER BLADE   TANG   RIVET   LINING or CASE   SMALL BLADE

HANDLE COVER

OPENING SLOT   BACK SPRING   PIVOT

A   KNIFE TERMINOLOGY

HOOK BLADE

C   D

PEN   B-CLIP   SPEAR   SABRE-CLIP   SPEY   CARVER'S   CHIP-CARVING

B   KNIFE-BLADE SHAPES

TANG   SHANK

SKEW END

E   FIRMER or FLAT CHISEL

F   SHANK SHAPES

KNUCKLE   SPOON or SHORT-BENT

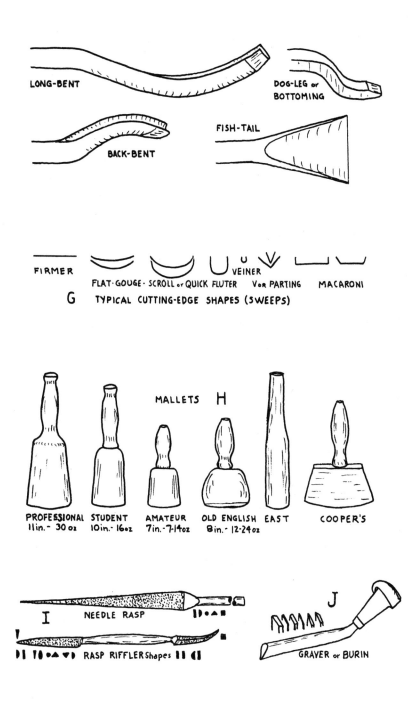

LONG-BENT

DOG-LEG or BOTTOMING

BACK-BENT

FISH-TAIL

FIRMER   FLAT·GOUGE· SCROLL or QUICK FLUTER   VEINER   V or PARTING   MACARONI

G   TYPICAL CUTTING-EDGE SHAPES (SWEEPS)

MALLETS   **H**

PROFESSIONAL   STUDENT   AMATEUR   OLD ENGLISH   EAST   COOPER'S
11in.- 30oz   10in.- 16oz   7in.-7-14oz   8in.- 12-24oz

I   NEEDLE RASP

RASP RIFFLER Shapes

J

GRAVER or BURIN

11

TYPICAL KNIFE CUTS

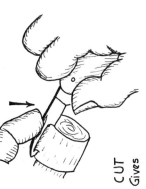

LEFT-INDEX DRAW CUT
Shaving + detailing. Gives
close control with more force

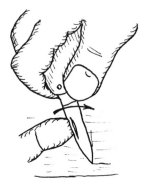

GUILLOTINE CUT
Adds force at blade tip.
Left index finger-or-thumb push

TWO HANDS

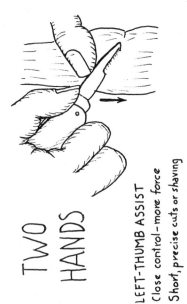

LEFT-THUMB ASSIST
Close control—more force

Short, precise cuts or shaving

LEFT INDEX-FINGER ASSIST
Shaving cuts. Work must be
clamped or held by left hand

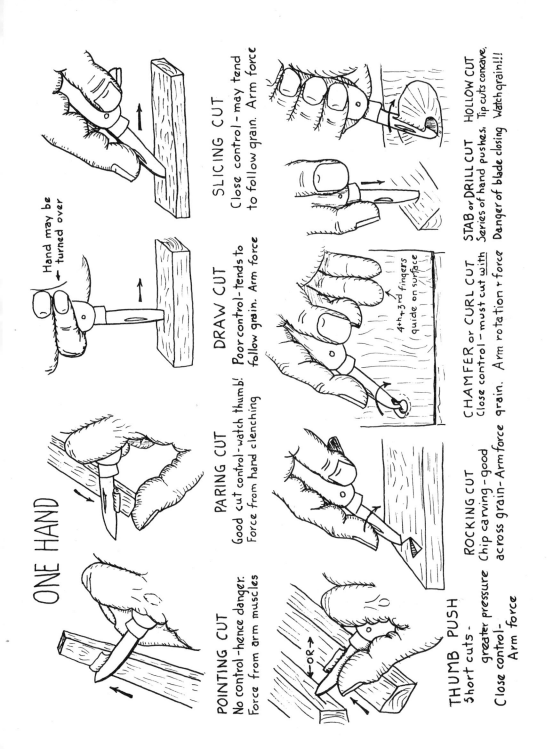

ONE HAND

SLICING CUT
Close control – may tend to follow grain. Arm force

STAB or DRILL CUT   HOLLOW CUT
Series of hand pushes.   Tip cuts concave.
Danger of blade closing   Watch grain!!

Hand may be turned over

DRAW CUT
Poor control – tends to follow grain. Arm force

CHAMFER or CURL CUT
Close control – must cut with grain. Arm rotation & force

4th & 3rd fingers guide on surface

PARING CUT
Good cut control – watch thumb! Force from hand clenching

ROCKING CUT
Chip carving – good across grain – Arm force

POINTING CUT
No control – hence danger. Force from arm muscles

THUMB PUSH
Short cuts – greater pressure
Close control –
Arm force

OR

Actually, even a razor edge is essentially a saw with teeth; the finer the teeth, the sharper the blade. Honing aligns the teeth; cutting an abrasive surface like those mentioned above throws the teeth out of line or breaks them off—and the blade is dull. A bit of oil occasionally on blades, pivots, and springs will help counteract rust caused by sweat, which can be highly corrosive. I know whittlers who carry their knives in oiled-leather sheaths for this reason. I also know woodcarvers who hone each tool before they use it, because exposure and time affect edge sharpness. I'm not that much of a precisionist, but *a dull tool spells trouble, and don't forget it.*

What tools do you need for woodcarving?
(Tool illustrations on pgs. 10–11.)

THE PRINCIPAL TOOL of the woodcarver is the chisel, either flat or curved. Flat chisels are lighter and often shorter than the more-familiar carpenter's chisels, and differ in that they are sharpened from both sides so they have less tendency to dig in. They are called firmers, and are available in widths from about 1/16 in (1.6 mm) to $2\frac{1}{2}$ in (6 cm) or so. The curved chisels are called gouges, and may range from U-shaped to almost flat, from 1/16 in (1.6 mm) wide at the cutting edge to about $2\frac{1}{2}$ in (6 cm). The smallest U-shaped gouge is called a veiner, and as its name implies, is used for cutting small grooves, for defining hair, and for very fine detail. A slightly larger one is called a fluter—again a descriptive name. The very large ones are primarily for cutting away waste wood and rough shaping, although they also serve in finishing large surfaces.

One tool cuts two opposed surfaces simultaneously—the parting or V-tool. It is shaped like a V, and is used in outlining, grooving and for many other purposes; it is the most difficult of chisels to sharpen and one of the most difficult to master for cross-grain cutting. Another tool, the macaroni, cuts three surfaces simultaneously; it carves a trench with flat-bottom and right-angle or outwardly sloping sides. A variant is the fluteroni, which cuts a similar trench with arcuate corners. These are rarely used and not included in most tool sets. There is also a variant of the firmer that is quite common. This is the skew chisel, in which the cutting edge is at an angle with the axis of the chisel, thus providing a point to get into corners and around surfaces. It is a versatile tool, as is the flat gouge—which may be a firmer with the cutting edge ground into an arc. The firmer tends to catch and gouge at its edges when pushed over a flat surface, and arcuate grinding of the cutting edge avoids this.

14

Wide tools, and some narrower ones, are tapered down toward the tang—which is the portion of the tool that is driven into the handle. These are called spade or fish-tail tools, and are very helpful in getting into tight places or for helping the carver to see what he is doing. The shank of a tool behind the cutting edge may also be forged into a curve so the cutting edge will be able to work in a confined place, such as a concave surface or around a curve. Depending upon the arc of shank curvature, such a tool is called long-bent or short-bent. A gouge with very short bend is also called a spoon. Normally, the arc is concave, viewed from the top, but it may be convex to handle a job such as forming the surfaces of individual grapes in a bunch or for cutting a special shape under an overhang; then it is called a back-bent tool. In present-day low-relief carving, there is little or no need for these specialized tools. Also, they are harder to use than straight ones, because of spring in the bend, and harder to sharpen.

Carving tools require the use of two hands, except tools that are very short or specialized, like Japanese tools, which have a long, thin, straight handle and a short blade. The standard tool is gripped and pushed by one hand, while the other guides the tool and controls it, keeping it from over-running or following a sudden split or breakout. This creates somewhat of a paradox, because the two hands work against each other to some degree. Note that I have not identified which hand does what, not only because the tools are interchangeable, but also because the skilled carver learns to hold the tool with either hand to suit the cut. This avoids a great deal of moving around or altering the position of the work.

In hard woods, the chisel is held in one hand, and hit with the heel of the other, or with a mallet. Thus, both hands are always in use, so the work must be held in some other way. Oriental carvers, who customarily squat cross-legged anyway, and do mostly pieces in the 1-2 ft (30-61 cm) length range, simply wedge the work into their laps. (They usually use mallets and chisels with no separate handles.) Large panels and large 3D carvings, unless they are top-heavy, usually require no holding unless very large chisels or mallets are used. The clamping method can suit the piece and be as simple as a nail or two driven through waste wood into a bench or board, or a vise. Decoy carvers, who do a great deal of turning of the piece, use a special vise with a ball-and-socket swivel that can be clamped at a variety of angles. A wide variety of clamps, in wood and metal, is available. An ancient device is the carver's screw, which is a long screw put through a hole in the bench or easel and screwed into the bottom of the work, then tightened under the bench by a wing nut. For small panels, a bench hook or bench plate is portable, convenient, and easy for you to make.

For work in harder woods, and for greater precision, it is advisable to use a carver's mallet, which is simply some form of soft-faced hammer. Then the chisel is held in one hand and the mallet in the other, so additional holding is still required. The traditional mallet is like an old-fashioned wooden potato masher, but it can have flat faces like a cooper's hammer, or simply be a club with a handle whittled at one end. Modern carvers have developed many forms of mallet. Some have plastic faces which reduce the noise, possible handle splintering and shock to the driving arm; some have lead or copper replacing the wooden head; some are even made of old washing-machine wringer rolls. This is a matter for individual selection. I have half a dozen mallets of various kinds, ranging from light to heavy, because I work principally in hard woods and use a light mallet even for most small cuts. With the mallet, I can control the force behind the cutting edge much more accurately than I can with just an arm push.

Carving tools are sized by the width of the cutting edge, ranging from 1/16 in (1.6 mm) to $\frac{3}{8}$ in (9.5 mm) in sixteenths, on up to 1 in (25 mm) in eighths, and in larger steps on up to the maximum, usually around $2\frac{1}{2}$ in (6 cm) for flat gouges. European tools are sized in millimetres: 1, 2, 3, 4, 5, 6, 7, 8, 10, 12, 16, 20, 25, 30, 35, and so on (1 mm = 0.039 in). The gouges are also usually numbered by the "London system" that measures arc or radius of the sweep; a firmer is No. 1, a skew firmer 2, a quite-flat gouge 3, and a U-shaped one 11 or 12, with the other arcs in between. For special tools, some suppliers use other numbers, their own catalog numbers, or simply show a cross-section of the arc of the sweep.

There are also many auxiliary tools, like straight and coping saws, rasps and riffler files, scrapers, hand routers and the usual carpenter's tools. (I use carpenter's chisels and gouges for roughing; they're heavier and cheaper.) Of these, the riffler files, which come in various shapes and sizes, some straight, some bent, with different surfaces at each end, are convenient for finishing in tight spots, over knots and faults, and on very small work. The adz and the axe are traditional woodcarving tools, of course, but will be discussed later as a special subject.

In some instances, you may have a choice of handle on the chisels. Usual ones are round, or octagon, tapering toward the cutting edge. Round ones are maple, ash, beech or boxwood; the octagonal ones may even be dogwood (which is preferred in Oberammergau, West Germany). Octagonal handles are less likely to turn in your hand or to roll on a bench. There are now some plastic handles as well, of course. My preference is for octagonal wood, with a brass ferrule at the tang to prevent splitting under mallet blows.

The customary way to carve is to stand up at a bench heavy enough so it won't shift. Sculptors who work on large blocks prefer a 4-legged stand weighted at the base with a rock, so they can move around it. Some stands have Lazy Susan (rotating) tops and height adjustments. Cuckoo-clock carvers have tables with heavy, sloping tops. I often work at an outdoor trestle table or indoors on a card table, and I sit down whenever possible. The main thing is to have a stable surface which will absorb mallet blows, plus a level surface on which tools not in use may be placed. My experience is that there will be a relatively small number at any given time, so an elaborate rack of tools at the back of the bench is not necessary. It goes without saying that good lighting is a must, particularly when dark woods like walnut are being carved, and that adequate ventilation is helpful. All of these things are matters of individual preference and size and complexity of work. You don't *need* a studio unless you teach or want to create an atmosphere.

As would be expected, Americans in particular have mechanized woodcarving as far as possible. Circular and bandsaws help shape blanks, routers cut away backgrounds, coping saws, power drills and sanders are used. Carvers of totem poles and wooden Indians have adopted the chain saw—with a great gain in speed of cutting but a great potential for making the user deaf and driving the neighbors insane. Carvers of small objects and/or very hard materials use hand grinders or flexible-shaft machines with shaped cutters and claim extraordinary results with them. Some have even utilized dental drills. My experience is that they are hard to control, chew rather than cut the wood, and throw dust and chips over a considerable area, so the user needs safety glasses. I have even met a few carvers who use pneumatic or electric hammers with fitted chisels. Like the profiler and duplicator, such equipment is primarily commercial. It may save time and effort in some instances, but hand finishing is usually required anyway if the surfaces are to have any quality.

Even the authorities disagree on the proper kit for a beginner. Commercial suppliers offer kits with considerable variety, undoubtedly based on the recommendation of some particular carver. Charles M. Sayer, who taught panel carving in particular, suggested four tools to start with: ½-in (12.7 mm), or ⅜- to ⅝-in (9.6 to 15.9 mm), No. 39 parting tool; ⅝-in No. 5 straight gouge; 1-in (25 mm) No. 3, or ⅞-in (22.2 mm) straight gouge, and ⅜-in No. 7 straight gouge. For relief carving, he added a ⅜-in, No. 3 straight gouge. H. M. Sutter, who has taught carving to a great many people during the past thirty years, starts his students with five tools, plus an all-purpose carver's knife: ⅜-in No. 3 straight gouge, ⅝-in No. 5 straight gouge (these two preferably fish-tail), ⅜-in No. 9 straight gouge, ¹⁄₃₂-in (0.8 mm), No. 11 veiner, and ⅜-in No. 41 parting tool. Note that neither suggests fancy shapes or skew chisels—at least to start. My best advice is to start small, with the advice of a capable carver if possible, and a clear understanding of the kind of work you wish to do.

Many carvers, and some teachers, make their own tools as they find a need for them, grinding tempered steel to suit, or forging the tool and finding someone locally to do the tempering. You'll need at least a flat gouge for roughing, shaping and cleaning up; a firmer for finishing and flat surfaces; a veiner for outlining designs before they are set in, and for emphasizing lines; and a V-tool for outlining, square corners and square-bottom grooves. A gouge or two with quite different sweeps and probably a skew chisel are the first additions, followed by gouges and firmers of different widths. A good rule may be adapted from that suggested to amateur photographers when they add lenses: When you get additional tools of approximately the same shape or sweep, double or halve the previous dimension. Thus, if you have a ½-in (12.7 mm) No. 5 gouge and want another of the same sweep, get a ¼-in (6.4 mm) or a 1-in (25.4 mm), unless you have continued need for one closer to ½-in. The same rule might be applied to supplementing sweeps; if you have No. 3, you don't need No. 4 or 5—go to No. 6 or even No. 9.

Actual carving with chisels is to me much less complex than carving with a knife, because the individual tool is less versatile unless it is gripped in the fingertips and used like a knife. There *are* a few fundamentals. Because the tool is pushed by arm power on soft woods, it must be restrained by the opposite hand to keep it from cutting too far, a problem which is minimized when a mallet is used. (I have never been an advocate of driving a chisel with the heel of the hand; I've known several carvers who irreparably damaged their hands that way.) If you are not familiar with hammering a nail or a chisel, you must learn to watch the cutting tip, not the chisel head. The potato-masher mallet shape is a help in this because it reduces the necessity for hitting the chisel head exactly square; obviously, the angle with which the chisel is struck or pushed influences the direction of the cut.

As cutting begins, it is necessary to adjust the angle of the tool so it cuts through the wood at the desired level—too high an angle will cause it to cut deeper and deeper, too shallow an angle will cause it to run out. This is particularly important with the high-sweep or U-shaped gouges. If the cut is too deep, the edges of the gouge can get below the wood surface and cause edge tearing of fibers. When cuts are started, it is advisable to start at the edge when possible, because if you cut to an edge, the chisel may break out the fibers there rather than cutting through them. In relief cutting, it is important to outline the desired shape by "setting in"—driving the firmer or gouge into the wood to the desired depth along the line, so that cuts made to remove background wood will stop at the cut line instead of splitting or running into the design. When a chisel is driven vertically into wood, it obviously must wedge the fibers aside, so it will cause crushing and splintering of fibers along the edge of the outline. This can be avoided by cutting a groove just outside the outline with a veiner, fluter or V-tool, so the edge of the groove touches the line. Then, when the firmer or gouge is driven in along the line, the groove provides relief for the tool wedge at the surface. As a matter of fact, in shallow-relief carving, particularly in green wood, it is often possible to get the required depth of background (called "bosting") with a deep fluter alone, leaving a desirable small arc at the bottom edge of the upstanding portion.

A gouge differs from a knife in that it cuts two sides at once, so that cutting against the grain is a constant problem, not an occasional one as with the knife or firmer. In a diagonal cut, one side of the gouge will cut cleaner than the other because it is running out of the grain while the other runs in. This is the major reason for keeping the blade very sharp—to minimize the tearing in angle cuts and the breakout when one cut crosses another. Grain is always a challenge, and in woodcarving one is likely to encounter knots and other faults because the workpiece tends to be larger. It is necessary, therefore, to work with the grain as much as possible, and to proceed with extra caution when working against it. You will find that a few experiences with splitouts and the like will train you to make adjustments for grain almost automatically. You'll still be tricked from time to time by sudden grain-direction changes, hard spots, and whatever, depending upon the wood and its source. I've run into bullets and nails deep inside salvaged wood, to say nothing of rotten spots or old insect bores that are not visible on the surface.

What wood is best?

THE WOOD TO CHOOSE may depend upon what is available, and what you are willing to pay for it. Many carvers salvage wood from old furniture, fallen trees, or along the shore of stream, lake or ocean. If you have a choice, what is the natural color of the bird or animal you plan to carve? What tools do you plan to use? Is the carving to be painted, textured, polished? Where will it be used or displayed?

As you can see, one question leads to another when you select a wood. If you are a beginner or a figure whittler, your best wood is probably basswood (also called bee tree, and similar to European linden). It is soft, white, easy to carve and hasn't much tendency to split. Ponderosa pine is almost as good, if you avoid the strongly colored pieces. Sugar pine, commonly called white pine, is a bit more porous, but also very good. Jelutong, a recent import from Indonesia, is like basswood. All take color well, but are too soft to wear well or carry much detail. Avoid yellow pine, which is hard and resinous.

Among other soft woods are poplar, which bruises easily and tends to grip tools, so is hard to cut; cedar, which is easy to cut but has a distinctive color; willow, which has a tendency to split; and cypress, which does not wear well. Spanish cedar, once familiar in cigar boxes, is a common carving wood in Mexico.

Many American whittlers have used local woods, particularly the fruit and nut woods. All are harder than those previously mentioned and have a tendency to check in large pieces, but they will take more detail and undercutting, give a better finish and have interesting color. Among them are pear, pecan, cherry, apple and black walnut. Of the group, walnut is probably the best American carving wood. It has a fine, tough grain, takes detail and undercuts, finishes beautifully, but frequently darkens when oiled. (It can be bleached with oxalic acid.) The mountain-grown Eastern white oaks are hard to carve, but can take detail and are inherently strong. Avoid red oak, because it has a very prominent grain and is coarse in structure. Oak has a bad name because of the cheap "fumed oak" furniture that was once all over, but it can be darkened with concentrated ammonia, or walnut-stained. Dogwood is very hard and withstands shock, but tends to check and is hard to carve.

Where they are available, butternut, red alder and myrtle are good for carving, particularly the first two. Redwood (sequoia) is durable, but some pieces have alternating hard and soft grain; this makes trouble. Sweet or red gum (also called American satinwood) is more durable and uniform than cedar, but tends to warp and twist. Beech, hickory, sycamore and magnolia are hard to cut and good only for shallow carving. Ash is stringy, but can support considerable detail. Birch is somewhat like the rock, or sugar, maple, which is hard to carve and finish, but durable. Many suppliers have soft maple, which is not a good carving wood. In the Southwest are found mesquite, ironwood, and osage orange, all very hard, inclined to split, and difficult to carve, but capable of fine finishes. Mesquite, like our fruit woods, is subject to insect attack. Holly, our whitest wood, is usually available only in small pieces. It is hard and tends to check.

Among imported woods, the most familiar is mahogany (which is not one wood but many). Quality and color (pinkish white to red brown) depend upon source and piece. Some, like the one from Honduras, is fine-grained, even though relatively soft. Cuban mahogany is dense and varies in hardness; South American varieties tend to be grainy and splinter easily; commonly available Philippine mahogany tends to be coarse in grain, but I have six samples which range from white to dark red and from coarse to dense. There are also other woods now being sold as mahogany, like luanda, and primavera, a white wood that cuts like mahogany and can be stained to look exactly like it. (Mahogany, when sanded, by the way, has a very light dust that travels all over a house!)

My favorite carving wood is Thai or Burmese teak, which is the best for exposure, does not rot, is not subject to insect attack, and does not warp or check to any degree. It is an excellent carving wood, which will support detail, but it does have a tendency to dull tools rapidly despite its inherent oil. The dulling is probably a result of silica soaked up in the marshy land where it grows. Chinese teak is red and harsh-grained, so the Chinese tended to stain or paint it black—hence the common opinion that teak is black. It is actually a light green when cut, which finishes to a medium reddish-brown, sometimes with slight graining. Another good wood is English sycamore or harewood, about as white as American holly, and available in wide boards. Lime and box, much used in Europe, are rarely available here. Both are hard woods.

Ebony, which comes from Africa, India, Ceylon, Indonesia, and South and

Central America, varies in color and marking, from a solid black (Gabon, Central Africa), to dark brown with black striping (Macassar from Indonesia, and Calamander from Ceylon). It is very hard, as is lignum vitae. In Africa and Mexico it is called guayacan and cocobola. (Avoid inhaling the dust; it causes lung inflammation.) Lacewood, briar, sandal, and satinwood are less hard and will take fine detail. All of these are more suited to carving with tools than with the knife. The same goes for rosewood, which comes from many southern countries and varies from soft brown through red and red-brown to a purple with other colors mixed in. This is a beautiful wood, but expensive, and should be reserved for pieces in which the grain and color are not competing with detail. Another fascinating wood is pink ivory from Africa, which was once reserved for Zulu kings. Anyone else found with it lost his head. It is very hard, and pinkish to red. Other woods like purpleheart, thuya, madrone, greenheart, vermilion and bubinga are also imported and offer a range of colors. All are expensive, hard to find in large and thick pieces, and hard to carve, but are, on occasion, worth it for their grain. (See the chapters on butterfly and dinosaur mobiles.)

The variety of woods available is almost endless, and my best advice is to start with the familiar and easy ones, then proceed cautiously to the exotic and expensive varieties, testing as you go. In general, the expensive woods should be selected for their color, grain, figure, or the like, not for pleasurable carving.

What size shall your carving be?

IN MOST CASES, there is no real reason why a carving must be of a particular size, unless it is part of an assembly. Size is usually dictated by other factors, like the available wood, convenience in carving, or size of tools you have. A miniature can be harder to carve than a larger piece, simply because your tools are too large, or the amount of detail you plan to include is too great for the grain or texture of the wood. Further, a miniature is hard to handle. Similarly, a piece that is overly large adds to the problems of handling and removing excess wood—you may find difficulty in holding the work, as well as in finding a place to display it when completed.

The scales of the patterns in this book vary; some original sizes are shown. This size ratio should be regarded as a general guide, not as a requirement. The patterns can be enlarged as desired by any of several methods (see appendix); only in rare instances is it practical to reduce size and retain all the detail shown. As a general rule, it is advisable to reduce, rather than increase, detail; whittlers in particular have a tendency to include so much detail that it tends to overpower the subject itself. What you are seeking is an image of a bear, not a texture that suggests a bearskin coat; or a rhinoceros, not a complex pattern of plates and wrinkles. A carving should be readily identifiable, unless you intend it for a puzzle. If a portrait of a person includes too prominent detail, we are immediately conscious of it, because we are accustomed to the soft curves in the faces of people we know.

Most of us have only a limited knowledge of animal anatomy, so we unconsciously put in too much detail "for realism." Also, we tend to think that all animals of a given species look alike. Many carvings of animals and birds are caricatures, or even crude, as a result. Some even have the joints bending in the wrong direction, or show too many toes or claws. It is better to avoid depicting claws, for example, than to depict them incorrectly. The same holds true for animal eyes and nostrils; they are differently placed and shaped than those of humans. Ear shape and position are similarly important—as important as the shape of the head itself. A sculptor uses a live model or good pictures of his subject; even a tyro must do the same if his design is to be believable.

Be sure you haven't selected a size that has details too small for your tools, or your skill, and that it does not include elements that your hand, and your eye, cannot execute. Be sure that the wood you have chosen is sufficiently dense and fine-grained for the detail you plan to include, and that the grain is not so prominent that it will overpower the detail, or indeed distort the appearance of the entire design. At least initially, don't make the piece so big that it is hard to handle or requires excessive waste removal before you can actually carve.

Particularly in three-dimensional carving, you may have to spend half your time getting unwanted wood out of the way before you can begin the interesting part of the work—actual shaping of the form. I must, however, in all fairness point out that the more nearly the design occupies the available wood, the less waste you have to remove (and in a sense the less wood you waste). Also, if you plan to sell the carving, a larger carving generally commands a higher price, even though it may require less work. People expect to pay more for something big, and less for something very small. This thinking affects inexperienced carvers, who will quote a lower price for a work of smaller size—and find to their chagrin that the time and effort involved are much the same.

CHAPTER II

Carving Animals

Suggestions for "different" subjects, poses, textures and finishes

ANIMALS, birds and fish offer a tremendous variety of designs. There are so many species, so many shapes, sizes, surface textures, poses. The possibilities for new poses, techniques, surface textures, and finishes are far greater than they are in carving figures of people. (We are one very limited species of animal ourselves, although we tend to forget it.) What's more, the typical observer has far less intimate knowledge of animal anatomy than he does of human anatomy, so he is less inclined to be critical of minor errors, or even of the exaggerations of caricature. All in all, this is a rich field for the carver.

Many carvers around the world even have specialized books on carving decoys, eagles and birds, but much of this is devoted to copying the living bird (or animal) precisely; in fact there are major awards for producing a decoy that looks as much like a stuffed bird as possible. There is, however, an entire field beyond this, that of carving birds and animals which are unmistakable but are not slavish copies of living ones. Take as a case in point the photo of four totally different treatments of the turtle. In this chapter are other examples, together with a variety of other ideas in animal and bird carving. My hope is that they will stimulate your imagination to try still others. You can go as far as you like, into great detail, or total stylization, free-form, caricature, and unusual finishes, with little fear of the nit-picking criticism that any carver of the human form is likely to get. We usually cannot distinguish individuals within an animal species, and in fact do not know anatomical details. This is borne out by general animal and bird books—in which sketches often widely disagree.

I have carved many kinds and many poses of animals in recent years, some small, some large, but most of them not the familiar domestic animals nor the familiar poses. These form a mixed grouping, which includes work done at various times, for various reaons, and in a variety of woods. Most effective in terms of observer comments has been the pair of long-tailed weasels. The stylized

Four variations of the lowly turtle, ranging from caricature to serious sculpture: the upper right figure is from the Galapagos Islands, the other three are from Mexico.

Two long-tailed weasels in mahogany. The weasel on all fours twists around the standing one. The polished finish suggests the slick coat of the animal. 4 × 10 × 10 in (9 × 25 × 25 cm).

Pekingese and the toucan caricature were both made from the butts of timbers discarded as scrap by a nearby piano company. The weasels were a serious effort at animal portraiture, and the musculature and poses were carefully checked with available references. The Pekingese, on the other hand, exploits the texture of the surface and the great plume of tail as well as the pug nose that characterizes the breed. Because the grain is vertical—that is, across the animal's body instead of along it—fluting with a flat gouge was relatively easy and did not generate the splinters that normally occur when mahogany is textured. Also, the tail has more strength than it would have with the grain lengthwise. The result is a piece that makes an excellent and durable doorstop, if nothing more.

The toucan is a composite or assemblage which resulted from buying a toucan upper mandible from a Cuna Indian in the San Blas islands off Panama. The body was carved in scale with the mandible, which was glued over a stub. Also, the walnut body was tinted with oils to suggest the garish colors of the bird and to carry out the tones in the actual mandible. This is a caricature, of course, as is the perplexed penguin.

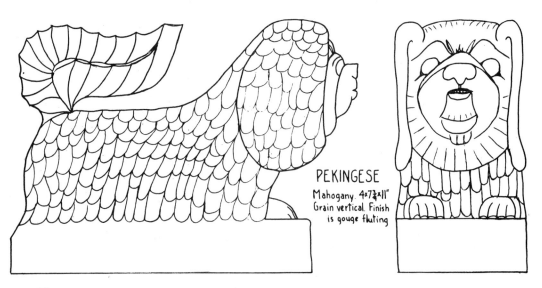

PEKINGESE
Mahogany. 4x7¾x11"
Grain vertical. Finish
is gouge fluting

TORO TOUCAN
Walnut, tinted. 2¾×6×16"

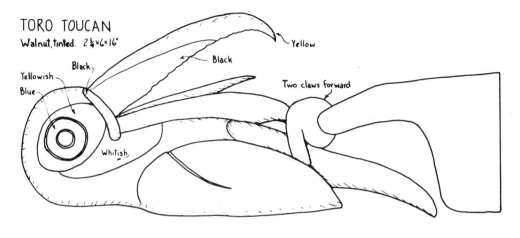

Yellowish
Blue

Black

Black

Yellow

Two claws forward

Whitish

Mexico

TURTLE, ARMADILLO & BIRD
Originals in black horn ⓦ white trim

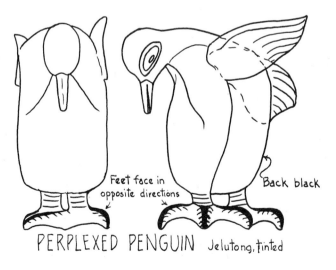

Feet face in
opposite directions

Back black

PERPLEXED PENGUIN Jelutong, tinted

The bear is a reversible piece, combining a stylized animal on one side with a caricatured troll on the other, so the exposed face can match the observer's mood. The bear design is taken from a smaller Swiss original I saw in Brienz many years ago, and I designed the troll to fit the same silhouette. (This can be done with various silhouette carvings, and converts them really into double-sided free-standing panels, thus avoiding the often dull rear view of a conventional in-the-round carving.) This piece is in butternut, a wood easy to carve, capable of taking the limited detail, and with a pleasing natural color.

BEAR & TROLL

Silhouette of bear is used for troll on reverse of a 4x6½x16" butternut block. (Some Scandinavians suggest that the troll legend is based on a bear seen dimly.)

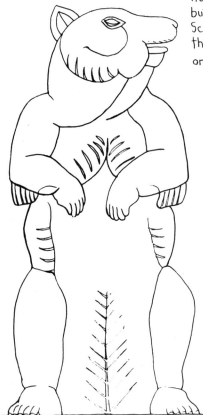

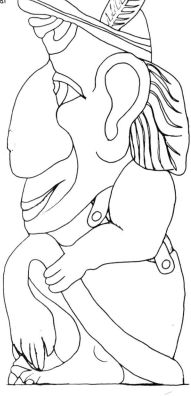

OWL (Granadito wood)

Earholes drilled
Eyes inlaid bone, wood centers
Beak bone
Copper leg soldered
Wire flattened

BOAT-TAILED GRACKLE

Eyes & beak inlaid as in owl
Top views
Legs as on owl

SWAN or FLAMINGO

Details as on owl
Leg length to suit

KINGFISHER

Somewhat similar in nature but considerably smaller are the pieces whittled by others. They include four caricatured birds in granadillo wood, made in Mexico, with copper wire legs and bone eyes and beak inset. The eyes are unusual in that they are drilled rings with black wood centers, inlaid in the wood of the head. Granadillo wood (also called granadito) is a mixture of dark brown and light tan, so pleasing effects can be obtained by proper selection of the piece of wood and carving the bird in order that contrasts are obtained on wings and/or tail.

29

Yellow

Orange

PUFFIN

Background pierced
between figures →

WOODCHUCK GROUP (for silhouettes)

Eyes are black crescents

FROG
Bass or pine with
green-gray finish
Card holder by
Fred Clark

The puffin poses I originally made in ivory, but they can be made in wood just as readily and lend themselves to tinting. These are fairly accurate depictions, but the bird looks much like a caricature anyway. The woodchucks were a silhouette group for the top of a breadboard, but can be done as a three-dimensional group, as a flat plaque or a silhouette carving, as you wish. The frog is a place-card holder if so desired, because his sawn mouth can hold a card or a message. Fred Clarke carved it.

All of these figures can be laid out on suitable blocks or boards and sawed out on the bandsaw, with details cut by coping saw. This saves enormous time in carving. The larger pieces are best done with chisels, the smaller ones with the knife. I have used a variety of finishes on my carvings in this group, each suited, in my opinion, to the particular subject. The weasels are varnished and waxed to a sheen, suggesting the smooth coat and sinuousness of the animal. The toucan is toned to contrast with the basic dark brown of the walnut. The Pekingese is textured with a gouge on all areas except the face and paw fronts. The bear is spray-varnished and antiqued with a darker stain in crevices. The frog is tinted green on top and lighter greenish-gray beneath, with oils or acrylics. The puffins are finished with oils, and the other birds left natural.

One of the most enduring of carved bird forms is the eagle, because of its association with the United States and because the bird itself is so impressive. I include three examples of eagle carvings in this group, because they are somewhat different from the norm and might not otherwise be available.

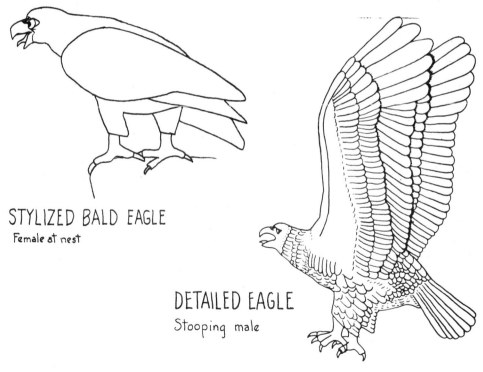

STYLIZED BALD EAGLE
Female at nest

DETAILED EAGLE
Stooping male

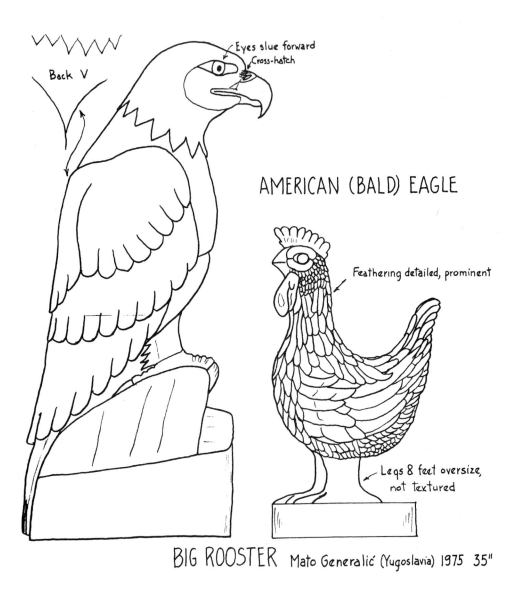

V V V V V

Back V

Eyes slue forward
Cross-hatch

AMERICAN (BALD) EAGLE

Feathering detailed, prominent

Legs & feet oversize,
not textured

BIG ROOSTER Mato Generalić (Yugoslavia) 1975 35"

I was also intrigued by a truly giant rooster 35 in (88 cm) high included in the Yugoslav naive art shown in the United States in 1977. In this case, the carver over-emphasized the feathering for effect, and even provided stumpy legs and

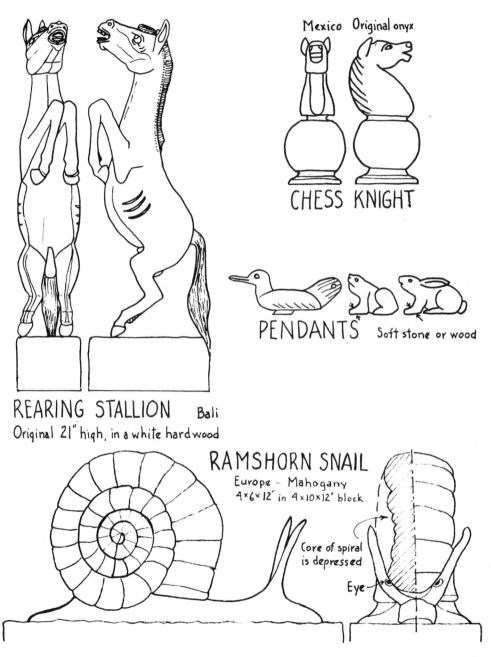

Mexico   Original onyx

CHESS KNIGHT

PENDANTS   Soft stone or wood

REARING STALLION   Bali
Original 21" high, in a white hardwood

RAMSHORN SNAIL
Europe - Mahogany
4×6×12" in 4×10×12" block

Core of spiral
is depressed

Eye

feet, seemingly a characteristic of Yugoslav peasant carvings of humans. The result is quite a dramatic bird.

Other examples of stylized, and perhaps caricatured, animals include three which, as far as I am aware, are not native to the countries where the carving was made. The lion from the Philippines is probably a result of tourist interest in lions, but it was designed exceptionally well. This goes also for the rearing stallion from Bali, a distorted but very dramatic pose. In sharp contrast is my ramshorn snail, which was an experiment in making carvings that can be placed on the floor. The weasels and the Pekingese are also "floor pieces."

In recent years, it has become the fashion for both sexes to wear neck chains with pendants; the more bizarre the pendant the better. Pendants are also used for chain pulls on light fixtures, curtain pulls, or just for decoration. Two groups of these are pictured, one small stylized animals carved in horn in Mexico, the other a duck, frog and rabbit in wood. Such designs can be carved from scraps of exotic woods and are interesting alternatives to standard or heroic figures. Blanks can be carried about conveniently and carved with the knife in almost any surroundings.

Stylized lion has exaggerated musculature and mane. It is about 18 in (46 cm) long.

CHAPTER III

Animals of South America

Most are sophisticated designs and works, from one small area

FOLK CARVINGS in wood tend to result from a happy pairing of forests and skill; either alone is not enough. Thus, in all of South America, there is little folk carving except in the Andes Mountains of western Bolivia, southern Ecuador, and northern Peru (which was also southern Ecuador until Peru won it, as south Tyrol was once part of Austria). Carvings from this high terrain, regardless of country of origin, are well-formed and smoothly finished; they are not primitive but are obviously made by skilled carvers to familiar patterns attractive to tourists. Subject matter is wide-ranging, from Indian portraits through religious figures to animals, particularly the llama. Both in-the-round and relief work are done, and mahogany is the preferred material. The exact duplication of design and availability in several sizes suggests profiler roughing for quantity production, but sellers insist this is not true.

Shown here are typical animal designs. Surprisingly, there are no birds. Included are a typical pair of primitive carvings—an anteater and an armadillo—from the Amazon basin in Peru. Drawings of three ancient house posts—over 1,000 years old—from Ica and Paracas, Peru, offer very sharp contrast to the more-refined modern pieces. There is also a small panel from the southernmost city in the world, on Tierra del Fuego Island, which is a quite modern caricature of a penguin done as a pierced carving, with body areas filled with a transparent tinted plastic—quite a surprise from such a remote place, but a useful idea.

Relief carvings tend to be silhouettes and fairly large in size. The llama (pg. 37), for example, is 11 in (28 cm) tall, the llama and Indian heads (pg. 37) are 13 in (33 cm). The designs on the cap of the Indian in the Peruvian plaque are exactly the same as those on the caps of a pair of almost life-size

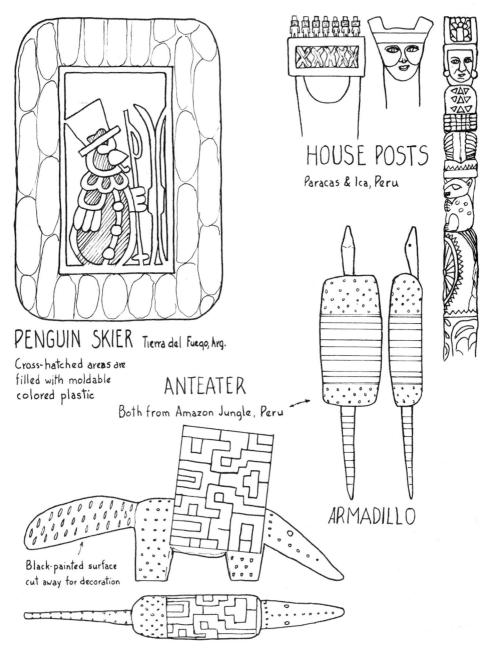

PENGUIN SKIER Tierra del Fuego, Arg.

Cross-hatched areas are
filled with moldable
colored plastic

HOUSE POSTS
Paracas & Ica, Peru

ANTEATER

Both from Amazon Jungle, Peru

ARMADILLO

Black-painted surface
cut away for decoration

Random veiner cuts

¾" wood

LLAMA
Ecuador

INDIAN & LLAMA HEADS Peru (Plaque)

busts I bought in Bolivia, showing again that tribal boundaries often do not coincide with national ones. It is also interesting to see that one house post has an animal figure very much akin to those on Alaskan totem poles, and that the posts are silhouetted, although the half-round hole in one and the notch at the top of another are primarily sockets for ridgepoles. The intricate line pattern on the anteater's back is typical of this area, incidentally; similar designs are woven into cloth, and have been for centuries.

The llama is the traditional beast of burden, and the source of wool for cloth and meat for food. There are three species, the llama, the alpaca, and the guanaco. Another familiar figure is, of course, the bull, but the dog and cat are conspicuous by their absence. (There is an ugly rumor that they are too edible to last long among the Indians.)

Two llamas flank an alpaca. The figure at the left is from Bolivia; the other two are from Peru. Woods and facial details are the principal differences. The llama on the left is carved with the base integral, and its legs are foreshortened. Detail is avoided on all three.

The Galapagos Islands belong to Ecuador, but are now an international sanctuary, so have only two small villages of humans. However, I did find one high-quality carving of one of the turtle species for which the area is famous. The islands have never been heavily populated and the turtle was probably carved by a mainland native brought to the area as a worker in the nearby turtle hatchery.

All of these designs appear to be the products of woodcarving tools, except possibly the Amazon animals and the bull, and they show gouge marks. The Amazon animals are painted, then carved, so the natural color of the wood is recovered—a technique that I have seen previously in Fiji and among Australian Bushmen. It is, of course, now in use in the United States and elsewhere for routing name signs in laminated or "sandwich" plastics. It offers ideas for carvers as well.

Composites of wood with other materials were apparently nonexistent, except perhaps in dressed dolls. The only examples I found are shown: the use of the transparent tinted plastic filler in the penguin skier plaque and the addition of a silver chain and bell on one llama.

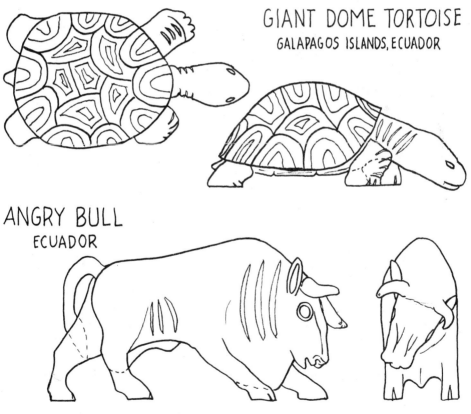

GIANT DOME TORTOISE
GALAPAGOS ISLANDS, ECUADOR

ANGRY BULL
ECUADOR

CHAPTER IV

Primitive Carvings of Mexico

Animals and birds are favorite subjects of folk carvers, who use what they have

CARVING is more fun, and pays better, than working in the fields, if you have the skill. That's the reason a great number of Mexican Indians have given me for their work, which they or their wives hawk in streets or hotel patios, or even along beaches. Many of these primitive carvings can be found in stores, which purchase them directly or through special buyers from the Indians. Some of the pieces are very good work and show both skill and imagination, but an increasing number show evidence of mass or hasty production.

Animal subjects are extremely popular among these carvers, and there is a great variety of techniques and designs. The figures do have an inherent strength and drama, and seem to exhibit an understanding of the animal depicted. A great many are caricatures, whittled of soft wood and painted; some are even assembled by nailing on legs, ears and tails, but others make use of the inherent shape of the wood, its figure or variations in color. One Indian who has gained somewhat of an international reputation told me that he frequently makes the same figure painted and unpainted, because unknowing customers prefer the painted figures, while connoisseurs prefer them natural. He, incidentally, produces a wide range of figures, ranging from traditional Nativity groups to highly imaginative animals. Some are hurried, some studied, some caricatures, some accurate portraits. Most are small and in-the-round, done with the knife, but occasional figures are large, and require chisels. This is unusual among commercial or professional carvers, who tend to have a specialized style and range of subject matter, but it is necessitated by the thinness of his market.

The examples shown here were collected to get a wide range of subject matter, techniques and approaches. There are some simplified designs and

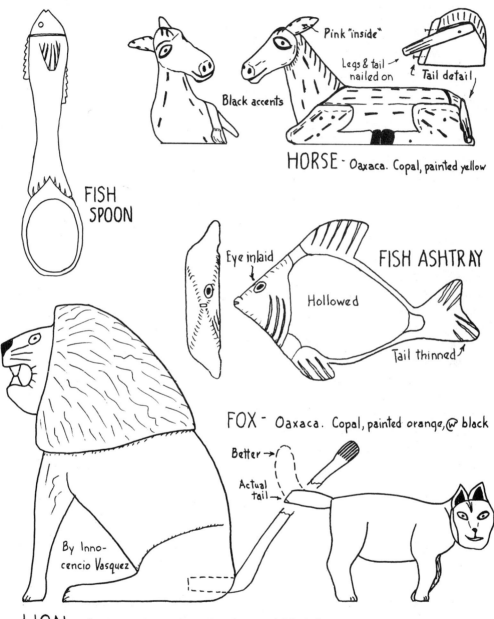

FISH SPOON

Pink "inside"

Black accents

Legs & tail nailed on

Tail detail

HORSE - Oaxaca. Copal, painted yellow

Eye inlaid

FISH ASHTRAY

Hollowed

Tail thinned →

FOX - Oaxaca. Copal, painted orange, w black

Better →

Actual tail →

By Inno-cencio Vasquez

LION - Oaxaca. Copal. Painted yellow, with black lines

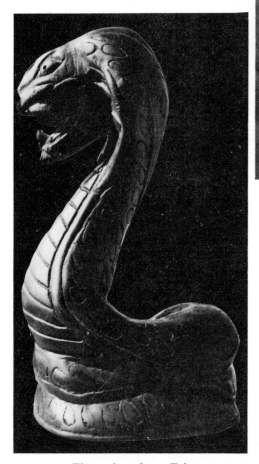

The light patches of granadillo wood are very evident on these two figures from Guerrero, which are hinged boxes. The top and base have been carved as a unit, then sawed apart, hollowed, and hinged together with a matching wood link. The hinge pin is a nail in a drilled hole and the eyes are inlaid.

This cobra from Tehuantepec, a massive sculpture in ebony, was produced by the same carver who made the monkey. It is an extremely graceful pose and very dramatic.

many shortcuts, the result of limited skill and training as well as limited materials and tools, but in general the carvings are less inhibited than many of ours because the Indians are not trying to achieve some hazy "standard" but simply to make what they see or imagine. They're not concerned with what other carvers may think of their work, because they usually work alone.

As might be expected, work is usually identifiable by subject, finish and technique. Thus the animals carved in caricature, assembled by nailing, and painted in clear colors are likely to be from the Oaxaca area. Animals made from the highly figured granadillo wood, and somewhat more precise in proportion, are from the state of Guerrero, and are further distinguished by inlaid eyes and polished natural finish. Decorated and shaped ladles, in soft wood and unpainted, come from Uruapan. Flat trays and ashtrays in hardwood, natural in finish and with inlaid eyes, come from the vicinity of Taxco. Examples from each of these areas are included here.

A great many of these figures vary to suit the piece of wood; there are no standard patterns or shapes—just a series of ideas which are selected as available wood suggests. Many are intended primarily as toys for children—another reason for gaudy color and hasty workmanship—and the major customers are Mexicans, not foreign tourists. Tourists tend to buy either very crude pieces, or the very finished ones turned out in several factories near Mexico City—the expected cowboys, fighting bulls, and sleeping mestizos. They pay higher prices without complaint. But, occasionally, really fine pieces will be produced in an unexpected area, such as the serpent, and to a lesser extent, the monkey, which were made near Tehuantepec from local, very hard woods. (Most of Mexico's finest woods grow on the Pacific slope, particularly in the south, so are not available to Indian carvers elsewhere.) Relief or panel carving is extremely rare, probably because of limitations in wood size and shape and in tools. In addition, primitive carvers rarely think of their work in terms of panels—unless they have been influenced by religious examples seen in churches or imported from more advanced areas.

The monkey (opposite) from Tehuantepec was executed in guyacan, a dark-green striped wood, by a South Coast Indian. It is considerably more involved than the usual primitive pieces, and shows much more sense of design. It is about 12 in (30 cm) tall.

CHAPTER V

Stylized Silhouettes Create Drama

The Seri Indians of Sonora, Mexico, make ironwood carvings which are not primitive

PRIMITIVE CARVINGS tend to be crude, over-detailed, somewhat fussy; only with sophistication and training comes suave, smooth, under-detailed work. Thus it is surprising to find carvings that could readily be called modern and uncomplicated coming from a primitive people. But this is true of the work of the Seri Indians, a small tribe which 40 years ago had decreased to about 300 souls (most of them on Tiburón Island in Sonora, Mexico), existing mainly by fishing. By 1960, they had formed a fishing cooperative at Kino Bay on the mainland with other Indians and many moved back there. In 1965, Tiburón was declared a game preserve, so the tribe, gradually increasing in numbers, is now in camps north of Kino Bay.

Early in the Sixties, José Astorga, one of the tribe, made the first non-utilitarian object in ironwood for a friend from Tucson—a paperweight. Next he made a turtle, then a rather poor porpoise, then a better one. These were decorated with pearls, brads, tacks—and got worse and worse as he tried the usual barrettes, hearts, spoons, bowls. Eventually he turned back to the sea and simple fish forms—and began to become known. Others, including his daughter, Aurora, began to make the figures as well, and since then carvings have become the major source of income of the tribe.

Earlier Seri carvings, including violins, toys, yokes and such, were made of soft woods; ironwood was used only for oars and bull roarers. Desert ironwood (Olney tesota) is the second-heaviest wood found in the United States (Florida leadwood is heavier). It is a hard, dense, dark-brown to black, striated wood that is capable of taking a high polish. It grows on the desert in southwest Arizona, southeast California, and down into Baja California and Sonora. The Seri technique is to chop out a crude shape with a machete and/or a large butcher knife, then achieve the form with a large file or rasp. Hacksaws make necessary slits. The piece is sanded very smooth, then turned over to women and children to rub with rags soaked in lard, kerosene or whatever else will generate a shine. Breaks are patched with resin. Recently, more sophisticated waxes are replacing the lard and heavy oil, so the grain is more visible. The danger now is hurried and poor production to meet demand, the usual degrading process that has affected folk carving all over the world. A further danger is a shortage of ironwood. But, at the moment, they are supreme examples of what can be done with a beautiful hardwood—folk art that can stand as sculpture in its own right.

If you undertake duplicating any of these carvings, remember that a major factor in their effectiveness is the wood itself. Pine or basswood is scarcely the material, and the hard gloss of a plastic finish will not substitute for the glow obtained here by a polish that seems to be part of the wood beneath. The West Coast is particularly favored in beautiful woods, and those of the Pacific slope and coast of Mexico surpass the United States in variety, color and unique quality.

If you are restricted to familiar woods, black walnut suggests itself, and perhaps woods with a decided figure like ash or butternut, or even birdseye maple, if you dare try it. In any case, the finishing is at least as important as the carving, particularly the obtaining of smooth surfaces. Features are suggested rather than carved: the eye socket is more important than the eye, the fold of skin more important than its texture. Of the pieces I saw, I was most impressed by the mountain-sheep head, which is a difficult exercise in shaping. It is,

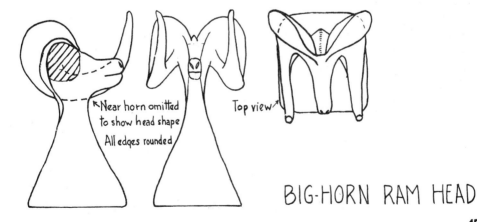

Near horn omitted to show head shape
All edges rounded

Top view

BIG-HORN RAM HEAD

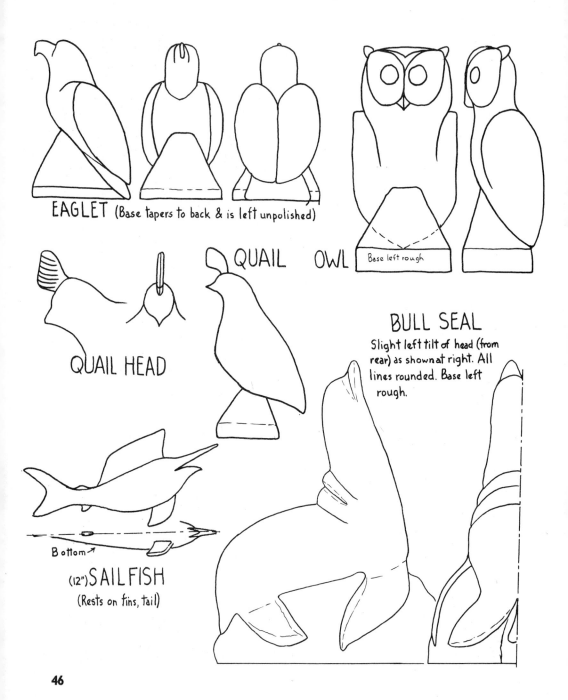

EAGLET (Base tapers to back & is left unpolished)

OWL

Base left rough

QUAIL

QUAIL HEAD

BULL SEAL

Slight left tilt of head (from rear) as shown at right. All lines rounded. Base left rough.

Bottom ↗

(12") SAILFISH
(Rests on fins, tail)

(*Clockwise*) *The eaglet is about 6 in (15 cm) in size. It grows out of a rough-finished base. The quail and the owl are severely stylized wood. No feathering is suggested on either. The owl is about 12 in (30 cm) tall. The seal, about 10 in (25 cm) high overall, is smooth finish over an irregular and rough base. Here the grain of the wood plays an important part in the effect, and the folds at the neck are as important as the head. The sailfish, about 18 in (46 cm) long, rests on its fins and tail. All sculptures are made of ironwood.*

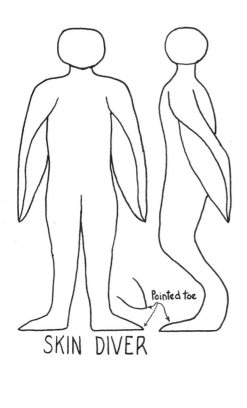

Pointed toe

SKIN DIVER

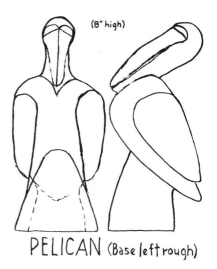

(8" high)

PELICAN (Base left rough)

incidentally, the only carving of part of an animal that I saw, and one of the few with a regular base. Also very dramatic is the seal, rising smooth from a rough base—a trick very much worth remembering.

Rather surprising to me was the absence of human figures, except for one stylized skin diver, who looks almost as much like a bird as like a human. In this figure, the line of the shoulders and arms becomes an extended fin, while the head is a simple, unadorned bump. The feet are extended, probably to suggest fins as well as to provide a stable base for the figure, but the toes are not wide across the tips, as when fins are worn, but brought to a rounded point.

CHAPTER VI

A Tale of Beavers, or . . .

How to vary a subject to suit a client's needs—rapidly

MENTION has been made of the infinite variety of designs that can be based upon a particular animal or bird. Here's a case in point. It has to do with an unlikely animal—the beaver. My experience with it derives from the fact that a particular client has sons who are members of a hockey club having the unusual name of Beaver Dam. Thus she has had need at one time or another for Christmas tree decorations, pendants and awards with some tie-in to the group. On occasion, she has given me carte blanche to provide what is necessary. Herewith are shown some of my designs, which may suggest ideas for you if you have a similar need. Many other designs are possible, of course, their form and function depending upon the animal and the need.

The beaver is not a particularly prepossessing animal, but he is appealing in that he goes his own way and lives a somewhat distinctive life. He is also rather easy to caricature because of his distinctive tail and bulky shape.

The first request I had was for awards for two volunteer hockey coaches—and they had to be produced in 24 hours! My solution was a silhouette panel of the "business end" or head of a hockey stick (sketched), about actual size— 7 in (18 cm) wide. Upon it was carved a beaver and the suggestion of a dam, as well as the name of the man and the season. It was in $\frac{3}{4}$-in (19 mm) mahogany, natural finish, and was made so it could be a wall plaque, or a stand-up or lie-flat desk ornament.

The next request was for Christmas tree decorations. I made a number, including a series of miniature skates of various eras, miniature shoe skates and typical skaters; but of most interest here were a hockey goalie, a player, and two other beavers. These were 3 or 4 in (7 or 10 cm) tall, the teak beavers textured with a veiner and finished in natural color, the hockey players tinted to suggest the colors of the club.

Another request was for a pendant to be worn at the annual dinner. For this I used a scrap of holly, which is a very white wood and resembles ivory when finished. Lettering was incised, then filled with stain, much in the manner of scrimshaw, and the whole varnished over, then waxed.

A further request, a year later but also for short-term delivery, was for a somewhat more ornate award, this time for a single volunteer coach who had led the team to the championship and also conducted them on an 8-day, hockey-playing visit to Finland. The championship was to be mentioned prominently, the Finnish visit somewhat less so, because some members of the team had been unable to make the trip. My solution was a larger beaver in mahogany, mounted on brass skates of the latest hockey style, on a Mexican mahogany base. Base dimensions were 6 × 12 in (15 × 30 cm), and the beaver was about 10 in (25 cm) tall, with separate tail inserted. The beaver was carved with cap and turtleneck sweater. On one upper arm was a miniature Finnish flag. Flag and cap were lightly tinted with oils in appropriate colors. On the base was incised the single word "Champions" and the date. The base edge was carved with a random pattern suggesting the logs of a dam.

The tail and hockey stick on this beaver award plaque are inserted in holes in the body, which in turn is mounted on brass skates set into the 6 × 12-in (15 × 30-cm) base. Body is not in the round, but flattened on the sides to reduce bulk and fit available wood. Lower body is textured and tail cross-hatched. Stocking cap pompon, edge of cap and pullover sweater are tinted with oils.

50

Award plaque for a hockey coach
of the "Beavers." Mahogany.

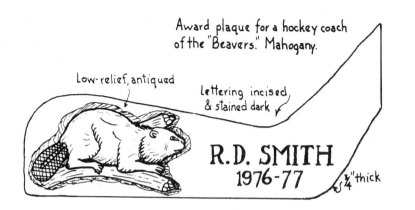

Low-relief, antiqued

Lettering incised
& stained dark

R.D. SMITH
1976-77

¾" thick

← ¼" wood

Beaver Dam

A HOCKEY MOTHER

PENDANT

Stick inserted

Puck inserted

Tail & skates
separate

BEAVER GOALIE

Tail, skates & stick
separate

Backs & legs of beavers are veiner-textured

Tail & chip added

BEAVER HOCKEY PLAYER

SHY BEAVER (Caricature)

CHAPTER VII

What a Tyro Can Achieve

Timberline Lodge, Oregon, was decorated by unskilled neophyte carvers

HALF OF OREGON'S 96,000 square miles (249,600 sq km) are publicly owned, largely by the Federal government, and half of the Federal lands are administered by the U.S. Forest Service, including the vast Mount Hood National Forest. So it was only natural that the Forest Service designed and built Timberline Lodge, the big ski resort 6,000 feet (1,829 m) up the south slope of 11,235-foot (3,425 m) Mount Hood. Further, it was built during the Great Depression, in the middle and late Thirties, as a make-work project for local people, some artists and craftsmen, but most trained on the site. The original appropriation of $250,000 ultimately grew to almost a million.

The basic idea was to spend most of the money on hand labor, using local materials and ideas. Even the woodcarving tools were made on the site. Much of the exterior of the building is made of local stone, with huge hand-hewn beams supporting the roof and interior floors. But the unique thing about the lodge is its many hand-crafted elements: 820 pieces of wood and iron work, 912 yards (834 m) of hand-loomed materials, 141 watercolors of local flowers. The unusual and powerful woodcarvings include panels in pioneer and Indian motifs, newel posts (recycled cedar utility poles) with animal-motif caps and beam-ends with animal heads. These are true folk art. All motifs are readily adaptable to smaller carvings. Such work calls for bold and deep cutting, with very limited detail.

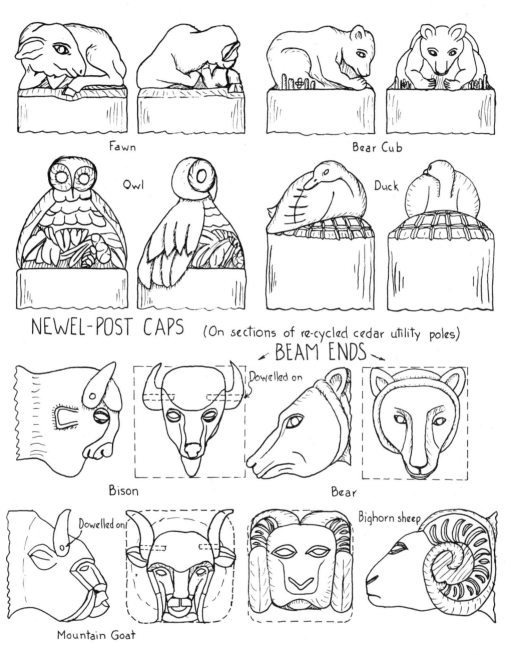

Fawn

Bear Cub

Owl

Duck

NEWEL-POST CAPS (On sections of re-cycled cedar utility poles)

~ BEAM ENDS ~

Dowelled on

Bison

Bear

Dowelled on

Mountain Goat

Bighorn sheep

CHAPTER VIII

Variations on a Theme

Even copies need not be slavish

THROUGHOUT HISTORY and in every field or profession, there have been two schools of thought, one stressing innovation, the other improvement. One worships creativity, newness, difference—in short, strives to produce or do something that has not been produced or done before. The other worships perfection, accuracy, intricacy—in short, strives to make a familiar thing better. One is concerned with ideas and dreams, while the other is concerned with reality.

There have been, and always will be, both kinds of craftsmen, both kinds of artists. Few of us are at the poles of this difference, but most of us lean strongly one way or the other. We have the whittler who strives to carve a longer or more complex chain, or the carver who tries to make a more lifelike or anatomically correct bird, or the sculptor who strives for a perfect copy of an ancient Greek figure. On the other hand, we have the whittler who creates new and sometimes amorphous forms of animals, the carver who refuses to duplicate his own or another's work even if he feels that it can be improved, and the sculptor who creates forms that are sometimes not even understandable from their titles. He is marching to Thoreau's different drummer, and the idea of sameness appalls him. Paradoxically, this difference may be the vital factor in making the individual famous as compared with commercially successful, a sculptor as compared with a craftsman. It is the innovator who wins prizes at art shows and exhibits, the craftsman who wins ribbons at fairs.

Famous artists have said repeatedly that there is no shortcut to art; it takes an enormous amount of practice, of trial and error. Only when the basics are mastered can the artist strike out on his own successfully.

There are many ways in which to be original, in which to vary even a familiar design; not all innovation must be total in concept. There may be newness in pose, in detail, in over-all silhouette, in arrangement or contrast, in texture, even in finish, for innovation is largely the meeting of a challenge adjusted to the abilities of the individual. It is a branching out, an effort to achieve something that is a definite step ahead *for the carver concerned,* an attempt to convert a mental picture into a physical one.

Most of us cannot hope to visualize the bird-and-flower compositions of the Balinese; our traditions and instincts do not seem to lead us in that direction. The cranes and snake pictured here are a simple example, in which the fragile bird legs are reinforced—quite frankly—with foliage, and the heads with crest and snake, without robbing a particle from the overall effect. The entire composition is fitted to the available wood but without being inhibited by it; there is no blocky and angular look. The composition flows upward from the base in lines that are not at all reminiscent of the original block.

For contrast, study the two Zapotec Indian (Mexico) efforts to reproduce the national symbol: an eagle on a cactus with a snake in its mouth. Neither carver was very skilled, but both achieved something which became part of a national exhibit. One worked almost entirely (except for the snake) from a single block, while the other was content to carve the bird, then mount it on a sawn assembly reminiscent of cactus. Yet both are strong and original.

The bull is in granadillo, made by a Zapotec from wood given him by a visitor from northern Mexico, and the polar bear is in sycamore chosen for the color and figure by an American carver. Each depicts its subject fairly accurately, but distinguishing characteristics of the animal and the innate coloring of the wood are emphasized. Contrast these in turn with the African animals on napkin rings, which are basically true to life, but adapted for a different purpose. These animals are miniatures, relatively speaking, and the silhouette is the important element in recognition. However, the carver avoided the ungainly effect of the over-tall giraffe by eliminating the troublesome legs.

There can be much originality in a frankly comic figure that brings a smile to the observer, as in the American goat and the Japanese owl with attached and rolling eyes. These, like the napkin rings, are made for sale, hence are simple in design, but they are different from run-of-the-mill objects. Another example of the same thing is the Noah's ark from Israel, which, like the owl, is assembled from unit carvings. This design has the advantage that the stylized ship can be assumed to have no deck, so that the body of each animal is

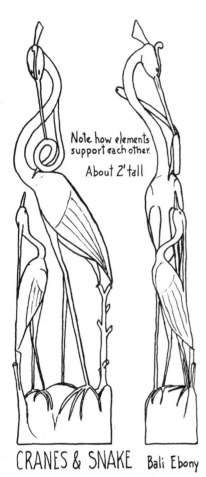

Note how elements support each other.

About 2' tall

CRANES & SNAKE Bali Ebony

Giraffe   Elephant

1½" bore

Kenya   Lion

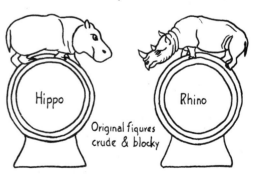

Zebra

Hippo

Rhino

Original figures crude & blocky

Owl has separate feet set on dowels →

Eyes inlaid

Ears & tail inserted

BULL Mexico Granadillo 4½" long

COMIC OWL Japan Cedar
Plastic inserted eyes have rolling pupils

POLAR BEAR U.S.A. Sycamore 5" long

COMIC GOAT U.S.A. Pine
Joe Rothrock, after Bob Horbison

MEXICAN INSIGNIA
(adapted for carving)

NOAH'S ARK A. Klein, Jerusalem, Israel

Animal heads & reed roof glued in place

⅛" reeds

Cabin

Keel

Hull

Animal heads

This unit dark↗

either within the cabin or below the bulwarks. The carvings are only the heads and necks of the animals, and they can be arranged as you wish about the composition, but the effect is unique and different. The same idea could be carried out in a fully 3-dimensional ark, with animals on both sides. The reed roof could yield to a single-piece one of textured or grooved wood, and so on, so that every ark could be an individual composition.

This suggests another idea that is relatively uncommon, that of using the same elements in a variety of arrangements, or—better still—allowing the ultimate owner to vary the composition at will, as children build with blocks. A series of building fronts against a common background, or amorphous human or animal figures that can be arranged in various ways on a base, are examples. One possibility of this sort is to provide flat elements with magnetic-tape or other "tacky" backs, and set them against a cloth-covered, sheet-iron plate or a felted board (not illustrated).

There are many ways in which some individuality may be expressed. The large-sized birds are two of my own examples. When I originally carved the "bug tree" I decided to crown it with a large cardinal. So I carved a fat, stubby bird from a wild-cherry log and put him atop an assemblage of more than 150 bugs—although the cardinal is a seed eater, not a bug eater. Some of my neighborhood "birders" were upset. After ten years, when the cardinal had succumbed to dry rot and the ministrations of friendly woodpeckers, I replaced him with a scarlet tanager, although I haven't seen one in my neighborhood in the more than 40 years I've lived here. My point is that you *can* cut loose and do as you like. You, after all, are the carver, the artist, and you have some license. Also, the bird need not be anatomically accurate unless it is being produced as a portrait. The cardinal was happily fat, the tanager has dowel-rod legs and no depiction of feathers. To anyone who criticizes, I can say that the tanager at least eats bugs, but I don't like him as well as his predecessor.

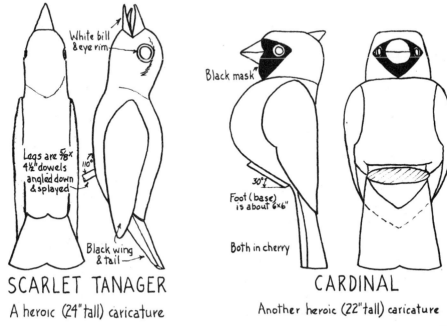

White bill & eye rim

Legs are ⅝×4½"dowels angled down & splayed

110°

Black wing & tail

SCARLET TANAGER
A heroic (24"tall) caricature

Black mask

30°

Foot (base) is about 6×6"

Both in cherry

CARDINAL
Another heroic (22"tall) caricature

59

Another example of the same sort of thing is the angelfish I chose for a pendant and earring motif in the rare and beautiful pink ivory wood. Because the wood has so much color and figure, I elected to make the pieces across grain, despite the long trailing ends of the dorsal and ventral fins. As it turned out, the wood simply cannot support such long thin sections, and even a minor bump of the pendant against something hard, or something pressed against it, breaks off the fin ends. Thus I have drawn an alternate design, which ties the trailing edges into the tail. It is not as accurate anatomically, but it is much more durable. This wood, by the way, is extremely rare still.

Another example of a fish design will reinforce my point about the permissibility of varying a design as it occurs in nature. Take the loaves and fishes. Both loaf shapes and fish shapes are generally known and accepted. But the man who laid the mosaic in Tabgha, Israel, long ago distorted the fish and showed only the ends of three loaves in a basket, to depict the whole biblical miracle of the loaves and fishes. The fish are not very realistic, although still recognizable. I have adapted the group for a barette or pendant and modified it still further. This can be done, and, again, it is artistic license.

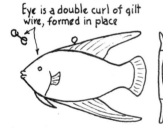

Eye is a double curl of gilt wire, formed in place

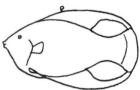

←Tail curves to one face, fins to other

ANGELFISH PENDANT & EARRING Redesign above is stronger, simpler

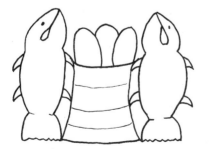

LOAVES & FISHES
Modified from the mosaic at Tabgha

As a final example, consider the doe and fawn (*ayelet* in Hebrew). I felt when I saw it in Israel that the legs were too heavy, and that they had probably been made that way because the material was stone. With the heavy legs, it is possible to saw such a figure completely from wood by sawing through at the nose, then gluing and filling the kerf later. However, the hooves were more nearly equine, as you can see from my copy of the original. So I modified the design to make the hooves more delicate, then went on to make eight further adaptations. All have a common ancestor, but they become less recognizable as they change. Three possibilities are shown here as my variations; you can certainly produce your own with a little thought. You will not have the same inhibitions or freedoms as I do, so your designs will inevitably be different. That is not necessarily bad. The point is that you can and should vary designs to suit your purposes or inclinations, and have no compunction about doing so. Sometimes, you'll improve the original idea in the process.

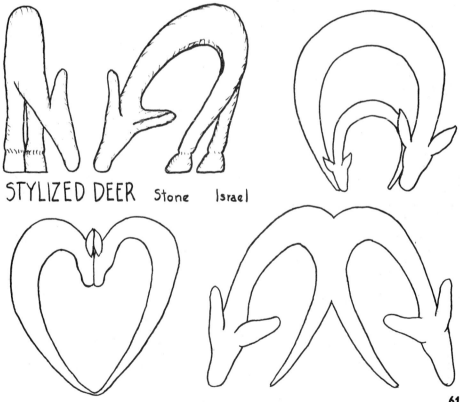

STYLIZED DEER   Stone   Israel

CHAPTER IX

Butterfly Mobiles and Ornaments

They show grain, and can be assembled of thin sections

BUTTERFLIES have long been a staple of decorative design (several are on stamps), but they are uncommon in woodcarving, probably because they are so fragile and so wasteful of wood if sculpted from a single piece. However, they do provide an unusual opportunity to display attractive wood grain or figure, exotic colors, and growth-wood and saw-cut variations because of the large and relatively flat wing areas.

Among the attractive wood-carvings you can make are single-butterfly curtain or drape decorations and three-unit mobiles. Other uses which suggest themselves are adhesive- or magnetic-backed units, pins, pendants, or desk ornaments, because these designs can be almost any size. I began with two fairly large swallowtails in purpleheart, principally because I wanted to experiment with variations in tone and wing position. My wood was 4/4-in (25 mm) finished, so I could get four wings from each blank, because wing thickness is less than $\frac{1}{8}$ in (3 mm). In this species, the wings are visibly distinct from the body, so I arranged grain to permit whittling $\frac{1}{8}$-in (3 mm) pegs at wing termini to fit into corresponding holes in the separate body. Also, this species has some white near the outer edges of the wings, so I drilled holes of suitable sizes, then shaped them with a long-pointed penknife blade. Wings were thinned along the edges to make them appear thinner and more delicate than they really are. The latter proved easier by rotary sanding than by carving because purpleheart is hard and resistant to shaving. Veins in wings were made with parallel knife cuts.

The color in the wood can be brought out by heating, and it is possible to control the depth of color in several ways. Wings placed in a small electric toaster oven will darken along edges and openings and in thinner sections first. Other zonal effects can be obtained by careful heating with a propane torch, but this is tricky because the surface burns easily. Oven heating can also be used—again carefully.

A butterfly's body is extremely complex in actuality, but it can be simplified into three major parts, the head, thorax and abdomen, the abdomen normally being about the length of the other two put together. On the head, the principal visible features are the antennae, which can be simulated with piano wire, often left with the natural curve of the coil, and with the outer end formed into a small loop. They may project from small clubs at the base, or simply from the head itself. The thorax carries all the organs of locomotion, including six legs and the four wings. It is actually segmented into three parts, but these are not visible unless the insect is dissected. The abdomen has nine segments and can be simulated as a cone, although it varies in exact shape from species to species. Also, the body itself can be small or large with relation to the wings. (If you want to be a purist, there are butterfly guides available.) But normally, bodies as drawn here are better than observers will expect. Wings can be separate pieces, or in most species can be combined because of the slight overlap. The upper wing laps over the lower midway of their length.

The principal aim is to display the varieties of wood anyway, so the wings are the crucial elements. I have tried to provide here the major variations in shape and size, and a variety of the possibilities in handling them. The monarch

The "look" of a butterfly can be changed considerably by adjusting the angle at which wings are set into the body. Note wing veining and shaped wing-edge holes. The higher the wing angle, however, the the more difficult is the balancing.

63

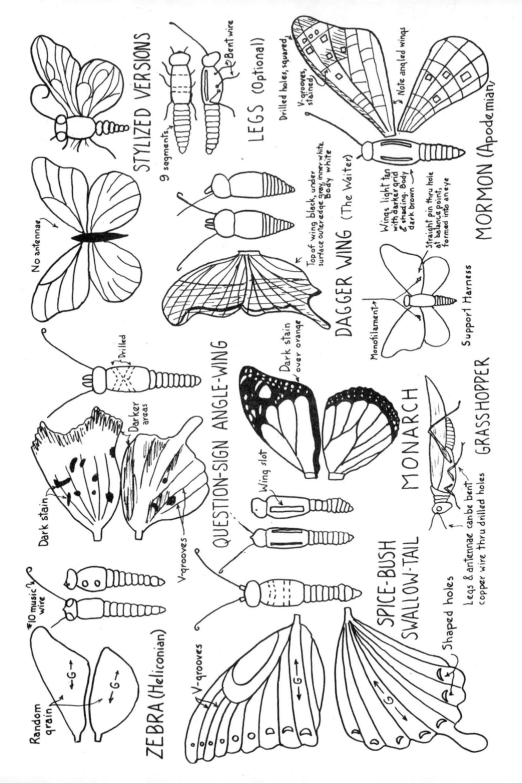

STYLIZED VERSIONS

LEGS (Optional)

Bent wire

9 segments

No antennae

MORMON (Apodemian)

Drilled holes, squared

V-grooves, stained

Note angled wings

Top of wing black, under surface outer edge grey, inner white. Body white

DAGGER WING (The Waiter)

Wings light tan with darker grid & shading. Body dark brown

Straight pin thru hole at balance point, formed into an eye

Monofilament

Support Harness

Drilled

Darker areas

QUESTION-SIGN ANGLE-WING

Dark stain over orange

Wing slot

MONARCH

GRASSHOPPER

Legs & antennae can be bent copper wire thru drilled holes

Dark stain

V-grooves

SPICE-BUSH SWALLOW-TAIL

Shaped holes

#10 music wire

ZEBRA (Heliconian)

V-grooves

Random grain

←G→

←G→

←G→

←G→

is such a distinctive and well-known butterfly that I made mine of pine and dark-stained the pattern over a lighter-colored background. In the case of multiple stains, it is advisable to give the wood a coat or two of flat (matte or satin) varnish before the stains are applied, to reduce the tendency of the stain to soak in and run. The same is true if you decide to paint butterflies in their approximate natural colors. Over varnish, color where you don't want it can be removed by wiping or scratching.

Because the wings are heavy compared with the body, you may have problems with any support for hanging. Balancing the insect fore and aft is difficult unless the wings are mounted relatively flat. The bent-pin method sketched is neat if you can find a precise center of balance and put the pins well out on the wings; otherwise it is easier to make a 4-point suspension, with a hole in each wing, so the insect can be posed at the desired angle front and back as well as side to side. Whiffletrees* for the mobile are made of #18 or #20 piano wire for the longer one, #10 for the shorter. Each whiffletree need be only long enough to clear half the width of the butterfly to be suspended at the higher level. If monofilament nylon is used for suspension, it is advisable to double-knot and glue when balance is achieved; nylon will loosen and slip if you don't.

All parts for these butterflies were made by hand, but wings can be band or jig sawed, of course, and $\frac{1}{8}$-in (3-mm) wing thickness obtained by planing or sanding. The best tool for shaping holes and veining I found to be a knife with hook blade. It is stiff enough to work any wood and is readily interchangeable with a standard blade for normal knife cutting.

If butterflies are to be used singly, you may want to add legs. These can simply be copper wire put through straight holes in the thorax. If the butterfly is to stand, glue the legs in position and splay them out to support it. If it is to hang on a curtain or drape, sharpen the two forward leg tips so they will penetrate the material, and bend them into tiny hooks. You will find that many variations are possible in wing position and angle of suspension, as well as in color, particularly if exotic woods are used. It is possible also to make butterflies simply of two wings glued together at an angle—with no body at all. The wings can be thin slices of burl or other figured areas, and backed with a pin. However you make them, butterflies are very pleasing.

*balance beams

CHAPTER X

Dinosaurs Make a Mobile

Use as many units as you like, and arrange them to suit the location

MOBILES can be interesting whittling projects for a number of reasons. They are flexible in number of elements, size and composition. Elements may be alike or different, and need not all be of one wood. A mobile can offer an opportunity to work, compare and display a variety of woods. Further, the number of elements is up to you. Having made mobiles of birds and fish previously, I chose dinosaurs as my next unlikely subject, because they varied so in shape and size and because relatively little is known about them.

Wood can be selected for color and figure, because dinosaur colors are not known anyway. I also disregarded relative time and size of species, so they are not in scale and species may have lived millennia apart. Some of the figures were carved in the round, but some were flattened to catch vagrant breezes and because only thin scraps were available. I used vermilion for the stegosaurus, jelutong for the man, rosewood for the pteranodon, mansonia for the sabre-tooth tiger, and an unknown wood from a Vietnamese crate for the trachodon. This was to test these woods in comparison with the teak of the triceratops, the maple dowel that gives a starting shape for the egg, and purpleheart for the big diplodocus, largest of the dinosaurs. Purpleheart, by the way, is extremely hard—somewhat like ebony, but not as brittle—and has occasional checks and faults. These secrete a black dust which must be cleaned out before gluing or filling. The wood itself is an ordinary brown, but lengthy exposure to the sun turns it lavender. Heating it in the oven can turn it anything from lavender to a dark purple, with thinner sections darkening first. Mansonia, by contrast, is a tannish-brown wood that splits and splinters easily, somewhat like some mahoganies, but it finishes very well.

Figures were finished without sanding, because the small planes left by the knife will reflect light. Figures were sprayed with Krylon® matte varnish to keep them clean, but finish, at least of harder woods, can simply be wax if you prefer. To suspend them, I drilled small holes at the center of gravity and glued in eyes bent from straight pins. The proper point for suspension can easily be determined by a little trial and error with a pin. Monofilament nylon makes a good suspension thread, but must be double-knotted and glued to keep the knots tight. Initial length of the nylon should be about a foot, to allow for later adjustment.

At this point, you must decide whether you prefer a wide mobile or a long one, and cut whiffletrees to suit. I wanted one that was longer than its width, so my top whiffletree was 10 in (25 cm) long, eye to eye. Piano wire makes good whiffletrees, because it comes off the coil with a good natural curve and because it is polished; this tends to delay corrosion. It is also, of course, much stiffer than other wire of similar diameter. I used #18 wire (0.041-in [1 mm] diameter) for the long whiffletree and #10 (0.024 in [0.8mm]) for the smaller ones, but any similar sizes will do. The wire may have to be sawed, then should be filed smooth on the ends and bent with gooseneck pliers. Eyes should be small and closed tight, or you will be plagued with nylon threads slipping out during adjustment and assembly.

Begin assembly from the bottom. The general principle is to pair off two elements of approximately equal weight, one tall and one wide, and differing in color if possible. The wide one must clear the support thread for the tall one, or be hung below it. Leave the threads long and double-knot or slip-knot them at the whiffletree, because single knots will promptly loosen and come free. Considering that the whiffletrees are relatively heavy compared with the figures, they will actually make balance easier. This is important, because even the usual postal scale will not read accurately enough to get exact weights of the elements and it is preferable to have the whiffletree hang almost horizontal to keep the threads it supports at maximum distance apart. Knot a thread over the center of the whiffletree and move it until the elements below it balance, then glue it in place.

Assemble the second short whiffletree in the same way. If your mobile is to be wide, you'll tend to balance two elements against two. If it is to be long, you'll tend to balance two elements against a single one on the medium-length whiffletrees. Other whiffletree assemblies are made just as the first one was. A particularly heavy element may have to hang alone, or be balanced by a light element hung from the center of a smaller whiffletree supporting two others. I did this with the man, the pteranodon, and the diplodocus. This also serves to

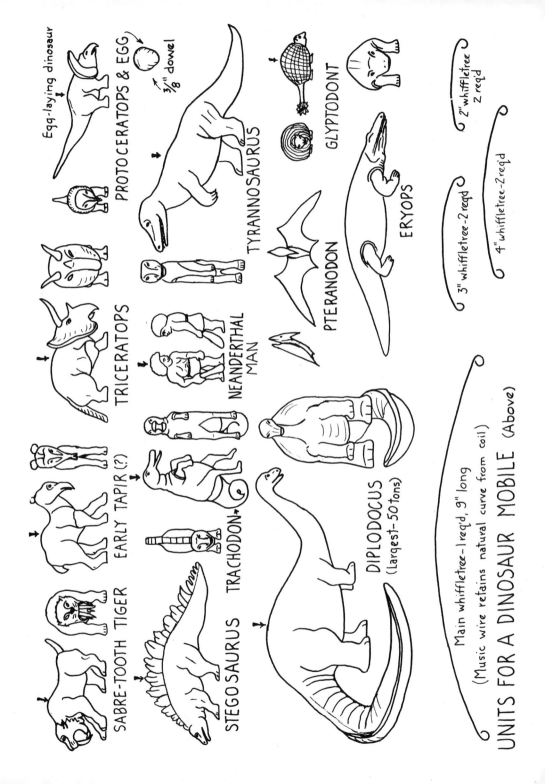

Egg-laying dinosaur

PROTOCERATOPS & EGG

⅜" dowel

TYRANNOSAURUS

GLYPTODONT

ERYOPS

2" whiffletree 2 req'd

3" whiffletree-2 req'd

4" whiffletree-2 req'd

TRICERATOPS

PTERANODON

NEANDERTHAL MAN

SABRE-TOOTH TIGER

EARLY TAPIR (?)

TRACHODON

STEGOSAURUS

DIPLODOCUS
(largest—50 tons)

Main whiffletree—1 req'd, 9" long
(Music wire retains natural curve from coil)

UNITS FOR A DINOSAUR MOBILE (Above)

UNITS FOR ADDITIONAL ARMS (Below)

These designs are adapted from sketches in "National Geographic" magazine for August, 1978, which show more details

STRUTHIOMIMUS (Running alternate)

STRUTHIOMIMUS 80,000,000 yrs.

ARCHEOPTERYX 140,000,000 yrs.
(Oldest known bird)

IGUANODON 135,000,000 yrs.

ANATOSAURUS 65,000,000 yrs.

PLATEOSAURUS 225,000,000 yrs.

TARBOSAURUS 135,000,000 yrs.

CORYTHOSAURUS 65,000,000 yrs.

Flat-gouge scallops

Spurs

ANKYLOSAURUS 135,000,000 yrs.

MEGALOSAURUS 135,000,000 yrs.

fill in otherwise open areas of the mobile and make it look busier in motion.

Hang the rough-assembled mobile from a ceiling hook or a projecting arm. I use a dowel stuck under books on a bookshelf at shoulder level at convenient height, and check elements for interference, as well as the general "look" of the mobile. Usually, interference can be corrected by raising or lowering one of the two elements that collide. You may want to shorten all suspensions to make the mobile more compact. This is a matter of taste, location and strength of likely breezes—the longer the threads, the more likely they are to tangle if the wind is fresh. My mobile is about 14 in (35 cm) wide by 2 ft (61 cm) deep. You may even have to change the length of a whiffletree, particularly if you have many elements in the mobile. When everything is adjusted, glue the knots and spray the assembly with varnish to inhibit rusting of whiffletrees. Also trim off loose ends of the nylon threads.

After about a year, I felt that I wanted additional elements in my mobile. Just about that time, there was an extensive story in the *National Geographic* about recent dinosaur discoveries. So I added two more arms to the mobile (one long whiffletree) to accommodate an additional nine elements. These were in additional woods: ankylosaurus in Virginia cedar 8,000 years old, iguanodon in maple, plateosaurus in redwood, megalosaurus in shedua, archaeopteryx in pecan, anatosaurus in walnut, tarbosaurus in chinkapin, corythosaurus in basswood, and struthiomimus in Port Orford cedar. (In the original group, trachodon was in pine, tyrannosaurus in cherry and proto-ceratops in oak.) I have sketched a running struthiomimus in case you want a long and narrow element, but his legs can be a real problem to carve unless you select a hard and largely nonsplitting wood for the figure. Assembly of this group is similar to the preceding one, except that in these figures I used tiny silver eyebolts instead of bent pins. Struthiomimus, by the way, apparently lived off eggs laid by other dinosaurs, so what he is clutching is such an egg, which was simply a long oval.

Mobiles can be quite simple. To make a "hostess present" in Mexico, I found a $\frac{1}{4} \times 1 \times 15$-in ($0.63 \times 2.5 \times 38$ cm) slat of pine on the street, and whittled five birds from it, entirely freehand and of no particular species. They were suspended from white sewing thread through holes drilled with a knifeblade tip. The whiffletrees were thin copper wire from a nearby electric-motor repair shop. Birds and their suspending threads were dyed in bright colors—red, blue, green, brown and gold—in the dye vats at a weaving plant across the street.

CHAPTER XI

Simplicity Is the Mark of "Brasstown"

Animal carvings from the Campbell Folk School

FOR AT LEAST the past half-century, the John C. Campbell Folk School, Brasstown, North Carolina, has been a stronghold of American folk art. It was originally established to teach crafts to mountain people in "Southern Highlands," helping them to develop their inherent skills rather than to impose inhibiting outside ideas. Thus their carvers have utilized the native woods to make images of familiar things, usually animals and birds, that are appealing and "natural." The examples included here were selected over a decade by Val Eve, herself a carver, who worked there.

The typical piece made at the school is simple, carved almost entirely with a knife, and quite realistic. It is not ostentatious or presuming, and rarely abstract or conscious caricature. It is, rather, a straightforward expression of an object familiar in everyday life. It is likely to be sanded smooth and polished, so the emphasis is on the wood and the subject rather than the carving. Only in bird carvings does abstraction creep in, which is understandable because birds move rapidly and in flight patterns that suggest modification of precise outline and

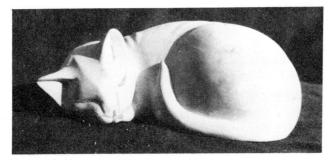

Buckeye is an excellent choice of wood for this kitten. A feline is hard to carve well because the nose is shorter than one thinks. Hind legs are very long, yet the body and tail must have sinuous lines.

71

DUSTING BIRD

BEAR Charles Church

CUB

LAMBS Hope Brown

SWAN
Ethel Hogst

DUCKLING Hope Brown

HOUNDS Jack Hall

form. This, by the way, is a common characteristic of primitive carving: it may be stylized but it is rarely abstract. Abstraction suggests the influence of outside, more sophisticated influences, usually introduced by art school-trained teachers.

Several of these Brasstown carvings are made in partially deteriorated wood, the markings of the wood and changes in color obviously being considered worth the loss in structural quality. It is possible, on occasion, to add considerable drama to a carving by incorporating such changes of texture and color into the finished design, particularly if the finish is to be natural, as in all these examples. In many instances, carvers select wood of a color to suit the design, and vice versa. Also, some carve woods wet that tend to split when dry. One carver there boiled walnut blanks for a half hour or so because he felt that this made carving easier. But beware of trying that on bigger blanks—they may split as they dry.

CHAPTER XII

Carving the Minotaur

Ancient Greeks believed he guarded the Maze of Minos in Crete

THE MINOTAUR is an interesting carving problem because he combines human and bull characteristics, no matter how he is made. I have carved him in low relief like a centaur, a human torso rising from a bull body, sprouting horns. The alternate is to have a bull head on a human body, perhaps with a tail added. After all, the minotaur is a creature of Greek fable anyhow, so nobody can say for sure how he should be designed.

To serve as a combined exercise in human and animal proportions, he makes an excellent companion piece for a centaur made the other way around, namely with a stallion body and human torso and head. Further, the minotaur torso can and should be compact and bunchy, while the centaur should be

Horn can be separate of contrasting wood.

lighter and more lithe. I made both in mahogany, with the grain running vertically. The minotaur block was $4 \times 4 \times 9$ in ($11 \times 11 \times 23$ cm) overall, but you may prefer a slightly larger base, say 4 in (11 cm) deep by 5 in (13 cm) square.

The front and side views are sketched on the block, which is then rough-sawed on a band saw. When sawing, do the back and right side first to avoid cutting away lines. The cut-off sections can be set back in place to provide support and guidance for the other cuts, the most complex of which are those across the front of the figure. They should be done before the left side is sawed, (see photo 1). Remove the extra wood from in front of the right knee and redraw the arm and leg locations, and the roughed-out figure should look something like photo 2.

Next, begin to shape the left arm and leg, including the shoulder and tail. Be careful to leave enough wood for the flattened ears. Also, take out some of the surplus wood between the horns, but leave plenty to support these cross-grain elements, as in photo 3. Now do the same thing on the right, in effect

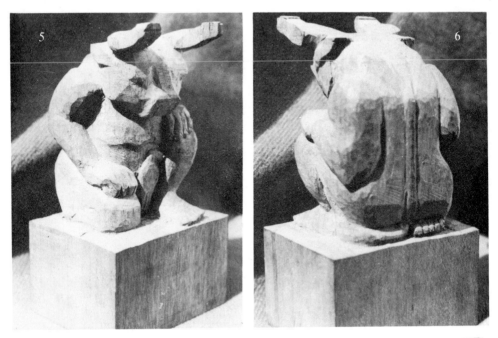

blocking in the body including the front (see photo 4). Shape the arms, legs, and tail, including the back raised spinal column (see photo 6). Shape the head, allowing for the flaring nostrils, ears and heavy brows (see photo 5). Shape the right foot, which is doubled under the right buttock (see photo 6). Don't forget that the toes, in this pose, are bottom up, but the big toe remains on the inside. Now finish shaping the body, then the hands, feet and tail, and finally the head and horns (see photo 7). The top of the base can be scalloped shallowly with a small gouge, and the eyes drilled for pupils or merely have a central dark spot on each eyeball. The finish should show tool marks—it helps accentuate the brute force of the animal. I used a teak oil finish and natural Kiwi® shoe polish and got just the degree of low gloss I wanted (see photo 8). Conventional wax would probably do as well.

A figure such as this should be blocky, rough-hewn, with not too much detail. He should not be sanded or polished, or he will lose force. Also, I feel that he should be in a darker wood rather than a light one, and without tinting or painting of any sort.

CHAPTER XIII

Carving the Centaur

A figure from Greek myth that offers interesting problems

CENTAURS (bull-killers) were an ancient race of men inhabiting Mount Pelion in Thessaly. They were reputedly wild and savage, and, as bull-hunting on horseback was a sport in that area, they came to be described as half-horses, half-men in later accounts, just as the Aztecs, when they first saw a Spaniard on horseback, believed horse and man to be one being. Suffice it to say that centaurs were generally considered to be evil in Greek myth, with the exception of Chiron, who was gentle and extremely wise, and had as pupils in medicine and the arts a number of the ancients, including Achilles.

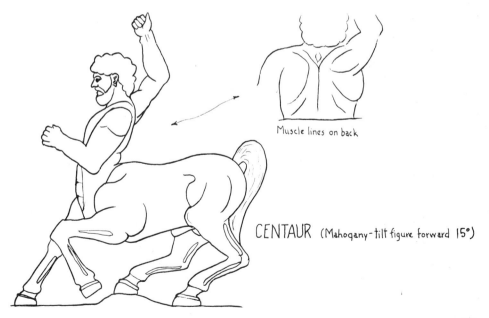

Muscle lines on back

CENTAUR (Mahogany-tilt figure forward 15°)

The usual depiction of a centaur is of the male, with a human torso running into the base of the neck of a horse. Amusingly, the human navel is shown, although the conformation would suggest that it be omitted. A little modern analysis would also suggest that the beast must have had two complete sets of internal organs and certainly must have faced some problems in deciding on a diet. Also, the centaur is often shown wielding a bow, but I have never seen a quiver or any other carrier for extra arrows. Thus I decided to show my centaur with the stabbing javelin and a couple of spares in the other hand, although his forefeet were probably his most formidable weapons. I omitted the human navel and selected a pose suggesting attack.

This figure is fairly complicated because the human and animal figures must be "faired" together to look natural. Some early painters and etchers avoided the problem by placing a wreath at the base of the horse's neck—which may also have been a device to avoid showing two sets of sex organs.

My centaur was carved in mahogany, from a block $4 \times 10 \times 10\frac{3}{4}$ in ($11 \times 25 \times 27$ cm), with the grain running vertically. The size was selected to fit the available thickness of wood. The javelins were made separately and inserted, so they could be removed for shipping. The base was slightly higher at the rear. Carving is shown step by step in the photographs.

The outline of the figure is drawn on the block, then sawed to shape (see photo 1). Note the forward tilt of the body, which adds interest and action to the pose. Because side clearances are close, waste wood is removed with a large flat gouge (see photo 2). Note the centerline drawn on the body and freeing of head and arms. Horse legs are freed from base by through-drilling and scroll-sawing, followed by chisel cuts (see photo 3). Head and extended right arm are formed first, for scale. Leg thickness and position are established, and center-line drawn. The upper torso is practically complete (see photo 4). Forelegs are shaped with chisels and knife, and back of upper torso is completed with musculature so horse portion of back can be shaped to scale. The rear legs and tail are shaped and horse torso is brought into proportion (see photos 5 and 6). Note that the tail flows back into left rear leg to reduce the danger of breakage. Musculature is refined, and javelins—$\frac{1}{8}$-inch (3 mm) dowel rods with separate whittled heads—are fitted into place. Face is refined and eye pupils drilled (see photo 7). Ground surface is gouge-scalloped to suggest rough terrain, and hindquarters are narrowed and shaped, as well as belly. Leg musculature is added (see photo 8).

CHAPTER XIV

Circus Parade and Carousel Horses

Nostalgia has led carvers into specialized areas

A NUMBER of carvers have been making models of circus wagons and carousel horses in recent years, recalling the golden age of the circuses in America from 1870 to about 1915. In 1880, there were more than 50 circuses on the road, each trying to outdo its rivals in the splendor of its parade, which was relied upon to attract crowds to the circus grounds. Larger circuses had extremely ornate and elaborate wagons, spectacles and regalia for the parade, at least one wagon reputedly costing $40,000 alone.

Biggest and most elaborate of the circus-parade models is that at Shelburne Museum in Vermont, which incorporates over 300 ft (91 m) of 1-in (2.5 cm) scale models, the equivalent of a 2-mile (3 km) parade—which no circus could ever mount alone. Models were carefully scaled from the originals or from photographs over a 25-year period, largely as the hobby of one man, with the assistance of four others at various times. It includes five bands; 53 bandwagons, tableaux and cage wagons; 400 draft, riding and driving horses; 90 ponies, mules and donkeys; 30 elephants, 33 camels, 14 zebras, 80 animals in cages, 60 lead animals, 20 clowns, 83 musicians, 170 riders, and over 130 other

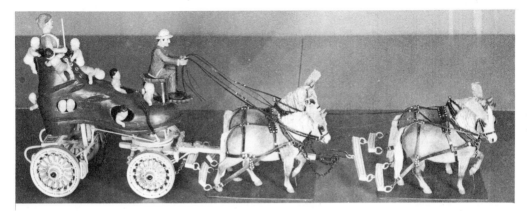

personnel. Wagons are hand-carved and painted; no two horses are alike. Pictured here are the Old-Woman-in-a-Shoe tableau wagon and the African crocodiles in tank-cage wagon, both drawn by buckskin horses, and a group of the carousel horses which are part of the same display. The parade is housed in a 500-ft (152 m) arcuate building built for it in 1965.

CHAPTER XV

Try Carving in Relief

Some of the basics—and some typical panels

WHEN YOU WANT to depict an individual animal or bird, the problem is basically quite simple—you make a three-dimensional image. But when you prefer a group, or a scene, or the third dimension must be limited either because of intended location or available wood, relief carving is the better answer. It is also a must for decoration on furniture, containers, panelling, frames, pendants, even non-flat objects such as vases, shaped pieces like wooden shoes or solid stools, and a host of other applications. Many of the carvers of ancient Europe solved their problems by carving in high relief, so that the third dimension for important figures or elements was practically normal, but this limited carving to fairly large furniture or mantels or the like, where the thickness and the weight could be accommodated. Also, problems of undercutting and support of fragile elements led to endless compromises and the necessity for many specialized tools, to say nothing of limitations in design and suitable wood. Even cleaning was complicated, and warping and cracking were common.

Carving in low relief avoids many of these problems but generates a series of others, as the ancient Egyptians discovered. Most of these have to do with the necessity of foreshortening the third dimension. In scenic carvings, there is the added complication of forcing the perspective. Early Egyptians avoided some of the difficulties by putting all heads in profile and by carving a scene in a single plane, so that their work approximated an etching or a painting with some moulding of the surfaces. It took them centuries to learn how to foreshorten the third dimension so heads could be turned without appearing to be mashed, and backgrounds could be sunken to create the effect of depth.

I mention all this because low-relief, or panel, carving is not as simple as it appears to be; in fact, many sculptors insist that it is much more difficult to do well than in-the-round carving. The fact that so many neophyte carvers limit themselves to in-the-round carvings of single figures would tend to bear out this opinion. A little experience with cutting away and levelling backgrounds shows that more skill and more tools are required, as well as more patience and care.

I have, however, always enjoyed panel carving because of its versatility in design and application, as well as its challenges. There is some surprise, even some shock, when one first learns that what in life is a curve may in low relief become almost an angle, and that depth must be simulated. Much of this will become apparent through study of the examples given here.

First, a few explanations. The Italians long ago classified relief carving as high, medium and low, plus inverted relief, or intaglio. In high relief, major foreground elements are carved in the round and figures in the background are likely to be half-round, so there is little foreshortening of the third dimension.

BREAD BOARDS
Netherlands.

Veiner lines

Round off

HERALDIC LYNX

Actual size of board ⅜ × 4 × 10½"

½" gouge scallops

84

Medium relief is a compromise, with the third dimension foreshortened to perhaps half of normal or thereabouts. Low relief, or bas-relief, foreshortens the third dimension to something like 10 percent of normal; rarely is background depth over an inch even on a 12×18-in (30×46 cm) panel, and frequently it is less than that. I have carved panels as large as 30×36 in (76×91 cm) with background depth of $\frac{1}{4}$ in (6 mm) or less. Also, in low relief, surfaces may be modelled as far as possible or many may be left flat, the third dimension being suggested by the depth of the background, chamferring of edges into the background, and various kinds of grooving and texturing of the surface. This technique is particularly important when the surface is to be used as a tabletop or as a wall of something that will be handled frequently, like a jewel box.

In trench carving, a technique invented by the Egyptians, the background is *not* cut away, except immediately around the subject figures, and some of the design may actually be merely incised lines with no modelling. This technique

Simple animal forms are silhouetted atop these small bread or cheese boards from Holland. Details such as nostrils, eyes and mane separations are done with a veiner and small gouge, the bottom scallops with a gouge.

gives maximum protection to the carving by surrounding it with flat surfaces and makes possible at least the indication of a great deal more detail. Also, it is much less work, which is one reason I use it so much. As a matter of fact, most modern relief carving is low relief, even though we have power routers to remove background, probably because of available wood-plank thicknesses and cost of material. Most modern panels will be $\frac{3}{4}$ in (19 mm) to $\frac{7}{8}$ in (22 mm), or $1\frac{3}{4}$ in (43 mm) thick, corresponding to what you get when you smooth 1-in (2.5 cm) or 2-in (5 cm) lumber. Reverse inflation has even further affected the euphemistically titled 2×4, which is now nearer $1\frac{1}{2}\times3\frac{1}{2}$ in (4×8 cm). Also, much modern carving is the silhouette panel, in which outer shape conforms to the subject instead of being a rigid square, rectangle, circle or oval. Some even dare to include pierced work, so the wall or light behind shows through. Even a wall-hanging in modern homes must be thin. A number of panels and a number of in-the-round figures have one thing in common: There's no place to put them, as any carver's spouse will agree.

There are certain advantages to relief carving which are partly psychological. The drawing can be taken directly from a photograph. Blocking out and removal of backgrounds does not destroy the entire drawing, as it does in in-the-round carving. A limited area can be completed at a time, so the effect of the composition can be seen, and enjoyed, before the whole thing is finished. The completed carving can be antiqued and polished with much less fear of breakage. The carving is a scene or picture, not a group of individually carved objects pasted on a board, as so many in-the-round groups turn out to be. In this instance, perspective works for the carver instead of against him—providing he has allowed for it in the beginning. (This is an advantage in working from a photograph—the lens will have put perspective in for you.)

Only a limited number of low-relief carvings are shown here, but they cover the basics, and provide some advanced and specialized situations.

Relief carving brings with it the requirement for more tools, the chisels and gouges, their sizes and shapes dependent upon what you plan to do. The veiner and V-tool (or parting tool) are practically essential, as are $\frac{1}{8}$- (3 mm) and $\frac{1}{4}$-in (6 mm) firmers and gouges, the latter in at least two sweeps, one shallow, one deep. All of these are used constantly in carving details, regardless of carving size. I find $\frac{1}{2}$-in (13 mm) chisels in the same variety helpful as well, plus a skew chisel or a knife for corners and tricky shapes. Because I usually work harder woods, I use a light mallet almost constantly. It gives me better control of the

This figure from a kubbstol (block stool) was made by the author from an ash log. It is an example of extreme foreshortening, because background depth is only ¼ in (6 mm), while the subject is almost 10 in (25 cm) tall. It is essential to create the visual effect of depth to separate the Valykyrie and the dead warrior across her saddle from the horse. Designs of this sort require a great deal of cut and try. Staining the lines and background helps to create depth.

cut than I can get with arm power alone. This means that the work must be held in some way. Flat panels of any size will usually rest without moving much on a flat surface, particularly if there is a backstop against which they can be pressed. Smaller ones can be clamped or even nailed down—through waste wood if at all possible—or placed on a carving board like that sketched in Chapter I. This will also protect a table surface, if you work on one instead of on a bench. The work may also be held in a vise or with a carver's screw from beneath, but this makes changing of the position of the work more difficult. Very small work, such as pendants, can be placed on a sandbag.

The size and shape of the work are very important factors in tool selection, of course, but I find myself using only about a dozen tools on even the most complicated work. For low relief, the bent gouges are seldom necessary, and I carve specialized shapes (bunches of grapes, for example) with a knife or simpler chisel. I have almost a hundred tools, but it is frequently much faster to make three or four cuts with a common tool rather than hunt up, and hone, a specialized one for a single-shaped cut.

CHAPTER XVI

Machine-Roughed Carvings

Israeli and German sculptors save time with profilers and saws, even on small carvings

MANY people have taken to power equipment for roughing, and even for finishing, what were once hand carvings, often not because of economic necessity but because we have been imbued all our working lives with the importance of time. Many amateurs who try woodcarving find it to be hard and painstaking work, so use machinery, as do many professionals, who find that hand work can be a low-priced commodity. Also, when you start with milled lumber instead of a log or branch, there is less inspiration, less likelihood that the wood itself will suggest a design worthy of taking the time to "feel" it out.

Camels in olive wood are blanked on a bandsaw and largely sanded to shape, hand carving being limited largely to head, hoof and saddle details. Even the chain links are sawed from a double-drilled block, sanded and assembled by splitting and re-glueing each alternate link.

The process of waste removal becomes more mechanical because the design is fixed. The product is "sudden sculpture," often crude in details and finish.

In Oberammergau, West Germany, a traditional woodcarving town, carvers struggle against continually rising costs by profiling most duplicates of larger work, and abandoning familiar pieces which do not lend themselves to machine roughing or are too easily duplicated in plastics or moulded compositions. In Israel, which gains a high percentage of its income from the tourist business, central "factories" rough out small figures like the camels shown here, then hand-finish them. They are sold in shops in the souk of Jerusalem, for example, some even equipped with the stage dressing of a lathe or other machines, a few hand tools and shavings on the floor. The proprietor may—or more likely may not—be a carver. But carvings are somewhat cheaper in the factories themselves, where I got these.

The traditional wood in Israel is olive, which is slow-growing, hard, an attractive yellow and brown, and highly figured. It is fairly common because some olive groves are being replaced by housing, but it is by no means plentiful

Turned panniers
glued in

Metal
chain

Simple, cheap, factory
version at left, hand-
detailed at right,
which is a 2-hump
Bactrian.

Surface is
reiner tex-
tured

RESTING CAMELS

or self-replacing, and there is very little other wood in the area. However, among the emigrés who come to Israel are artists and craftsmen from many other countries, and these are trying to continue and develop their particular skills. Thus one finds pieces like the bear, hedgehog and fox made by a German immigrant, and the ibex in cow bone, made by a Russian emigré. (He has produced a number of other pieces in the same material, some quite complex, but his market is limited because tourists tend to buy souvenirs rather than art. Bone is not nearly as susceptible to machine production as is wood.)

The German emigré has designed his pieces so that most of the heavy work is done on a lathe. The hansa carving from Sri Lanka (formerly Ceylon), can also be turned in a lathe, including the shallow V of the outer border and moulding circles, always difficult to hand carve. Then the background can be bosted (sunken) with a small router, leaving the carving of the two-headed bird and the leaves as the hand work. It is also possible to do some portions of the feather-texturing with a stamp that makes several of the small arcs at a time. (This is not the way the original was made. It bears all the signs of being hand-textured.)

There are rationalizations for machine roughing beyond the time saving. The long legs of many animals are an onerous carving chore, so production time and the danger of breakage can both be vastly reduced by sawing out silhouette blanks. The Israeli camels are an excellent example, because not only are the silhouettes bandsawed but also the wood between the legs. Panniers, saddle components and lead chains are made separately and put on, the gross-linked wooden lead chains being ridiculously proportioned, but strongly traditional. Also, much of the forming is done on a sander or with a rasp, and the eyes are formed complete with a special cutter. Study the differences in detailing and texturing of the two resting camels to see how much can be done by machine. The simple version sells for a pittance; the elaborately detailed hand-made one costs six times as much.

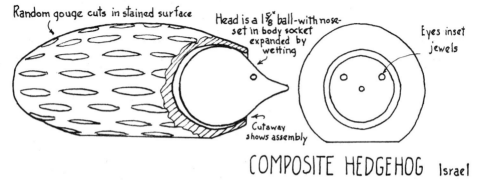

Random gouge cuts in stained surface

Head is a 1⅞" ball-with nose-set in body socket expanded by wetting

Eyes inset jewels

Cutaway shows assembly

COMPOSITE HEDGEHOG Israel

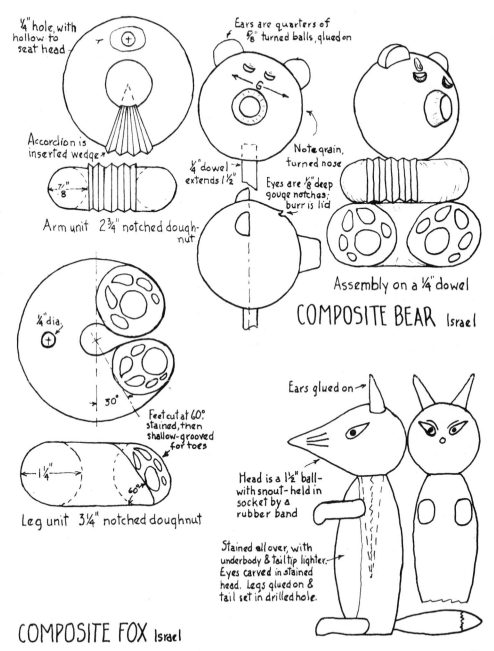

1/4" hole, with hollow to seat head

Accordion is inserted wedge

Arm unit 2 3/4" notched dough-nut

7/8"

Ears are quarters of 5/8" turned balls, glued on

G

1/4" dowel extends 1 1/2"

Note grain, turned nose

Eyes are 1/8" deep gouge notches; burr is lid

Assembly on a 1/4" dowel

COMPOSITE BEAR Israel

1/4" dia.

30°

Feet cut at 60°, stained, then shallow-grooved for toes

1 1/4"

60°

Leg unit 3 1/4" notched doughnut

Ears glued on →

Head is a 1 1/2" ball with snout—held in socket by a rubber band

Stained all over, with underbody & tailtip lighter. Eyes carved in stained head. Legs glued on & tail set in drilled hole.

COMPOSITE FOX Israel

The ibis and the duck are interesting because of another shortcut. Body shape is the same, but various species are suggested by altering neck and leg lengths and positions. This standardization makes preparation of blanks quite simple.

Because some animals are so familiar in general outline, it is possible to conventionalize or even alter or distort that outline slightly and still produce a recognizable animal. It is, perhaps, a form of caricature. This is true of the very blocky cat card-holder, which is square in cross-section and obviously sawed to shape, then sanded. Carving is minimal, because not even the features are outlined, but the silhouette, plus the slight narrowing at the nose, creates an unmistakable cat, even though its tail is the full width of the body and no

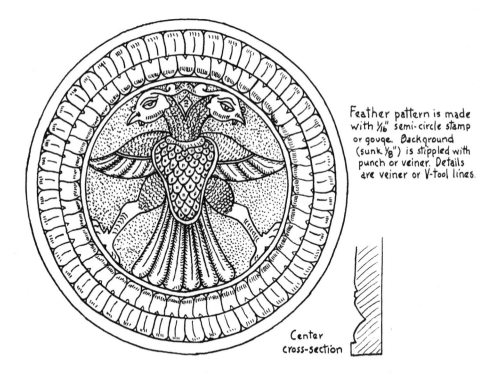

Feather pattern is made with 1/16" semi-circle stamp or gouge. Background (sunk 1/8") is stippled with punch or veiner. Details are veiner or V-tool lines.

Center cross-section

HANSA (Sacred Goose)   Sri Lanka Craftsmen
Surrounded by petals of the lotus (Pala-Petha). A traditional design, carved in a pre-turned piece of 5/8" hard, white wood.

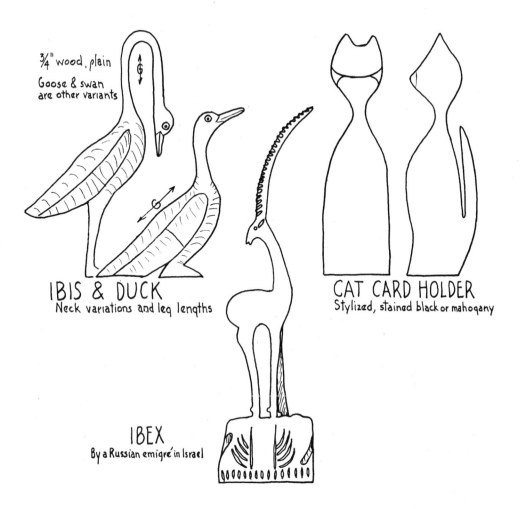

¾" wood, plain

Goose & swan
are other variants

IBIS & DUCK
Neck variations and leg lengths

CAT CARD HOLDER
Stylized, stained black or mahogany

IBEX
By a Russian emigré in Israel

modelling is done. Such a piece can be turned out by the dozen on a band saw, and be finished with a sander and staining.

The age-old skill of working ivory persists in the face of declining—almost nonexistent—stocks of the raw material. Many ivory carvers are turning to cow-leg bone as a substitute, as carvers did many years ago in Bali, where ivory is not readily available. The ibex is made in one wall of the bone and is jig-sawed to shape, with indentations of the horn and surface decoration on the base done with a flexible-shaft cutter or grinder.

93

CHAPTER XVII

Greek Peasant Carvings

Classical sculptural skills are gone, but folk art remains

WITH ITS CONSIDERABLE TRADITION in sculpture, one would assume that wood-carving would be common in modern Greece as well. Actually, even carving in stone is uncommon, and practically all of that is copied from classical models. The explanation that Greeks give is that wood is scarce, but in Israel, where the same statement is even truer, there is a great deal of carving. The practical answer is probably that the Israelis have built the craft, while the Greeks have lost it.

There are a few exceptions, but most of these appear to be not Greek as much as they are Thessalonian, because items on the mainland are peasant instruments and tools, decorated with chip carving and its variations, and they come from rural northern and mountainous areas. I described a shepherd's crook and a flute from that area in earlier books of mine. In several days of scouring Athens shops, I found one shepherd's crook and one pipe, neither as good as those I had, but described as "antiques" and thus ridiculously high in price.

Typical of the northern areas is the one-stringed *lyra* I have sketched here, well-made and carefully carved by a man now reportedly dead. This is a single piece of wood and well-finished, and is a traditional design and shape. Forming the body is the work of several days with primitive tools, and the decoration is a lengthy and painstaking process as well. The design could readily be made two-stringed to increase musical range and allow for chords, but this was never done, apparently. One-piece shepherd's pipes from the same area are usually multiple-key, having two to four flutes fanning out from the mouthpiece.

Somewhat more utilitarian, and far simpler, is the nutcracker in the shape

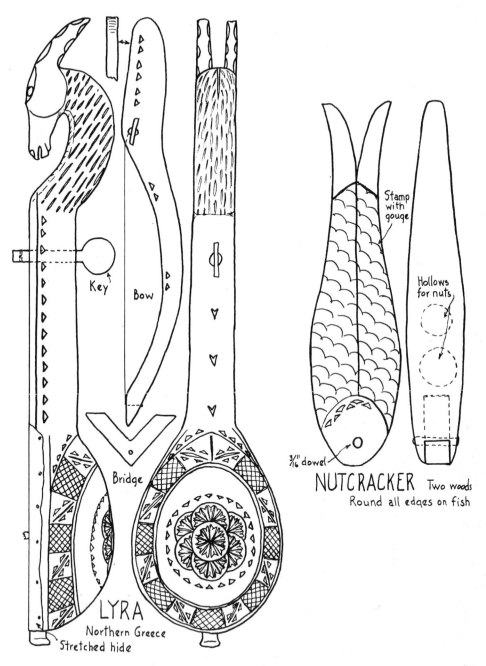

Key

Bow

Bridge

LYRA
Northern Greece
Stretched hide

Stamp
with
gouge

Hollows
for nuts

3/16" dowel

O

NUTCRACKER Two woods
Round all edges on fish

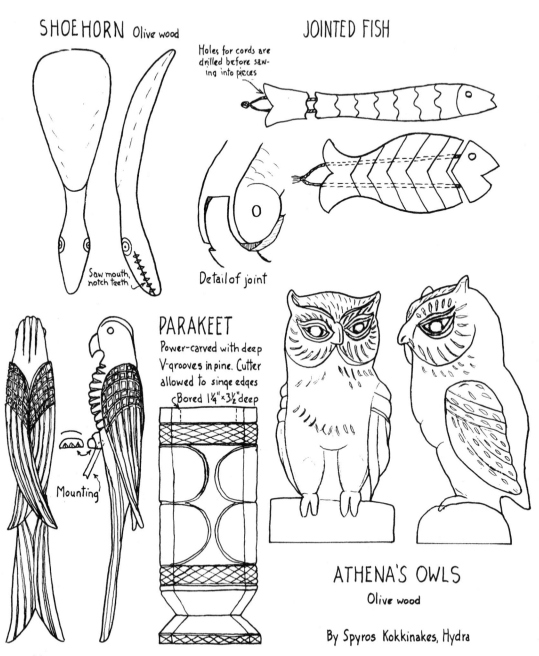

SHOEHORN Olive wood

JOINTED FISH

Holes for cords are drilled before sawing into pieces

Saw mouth, notch teeth

Detail of joint

PARAKEET

Power-carved with deep V-grooves in pine. Cutter allowed to singe edges
Bored 1¼" x 3½" deep

Mounting

ATHENA'S OWLS

Olive wood

By Spyros Kokkinakes, Hydra

96

of a fish. This is obviously sawed to shape and finished, including the joint, before the decoration is added. Because the wood is olive, the scales can be represented by simply stamping with a small gouge; the lines show quite clearly against the polished wood without actual cutting. Also, a dark stain can be applied and quickly wiped off to leave the color in the depressions. It is important to carve shallow, circular or oval "nests" for nuts between the jaws, to prevent the nut from squeezing out to the side and the meat from being crushed when the shell cracks.

There are occasional "different" carved pieces, which I found on the Greek islands in small local shops. All were of olive or other local woods. The shoehorn is a simple design, probably very old and certainly primitive. The principal problem is to use a wood that has sufficient strength in cross section to be carved thin enough for the horn. Olive wood splits and has a tendency to splinter. Maple, for example, would be better.

The jointed fish suggests a number of possibilities for other designs, although it does involve the problem of small-diameter drilling for almost its total length, and small-diameter drills are also correspondingly short. The holes can be drilled by brazing a shank on the drill bit, or by drilling to available depth, then cutting off sections until the bottoms of the holes are reached, making certain that drill "pits" are left in the stub to provide guides for the next drilling step. Assembly cords are glued into the heads. The principle can of course be applied to articulate snakes, lizards, and some birds.

The parakeet is a quite modern design, and much of the work can be done with power tools if desired. The shape is relatively simple, and the decoration entirely V-grooves, stained or singed by a rotary power cutter for an "antique" effect. A piece like this can be quite crude and still be effective.

The owl designs, made in olive wood on the island of Hydra, are unusually good, in my opinion. Owls were sacred to the goddess Athena, so owl motifs appear in a variety of Greek products, from pottery to wearing apparel, but these are free-standing figures. The carver "is quite old," so that figures like this will not be available much longer. One of the virtues of the design is that the carver avoided excruciating detail—every feather is *not* delineated; the lines suggest only general areas and directions.

CHAPTER XVIII

How Much Modelling and Texturing?

Partial answers to these basic questions, with examples

IN INDIA, and in China to a lesser degree, it was customary to cover the entire surface of a woodcarving with decoration, particularly if it was a panel in relief. In Italy, the tendency was to cover as much as 80 percent of the surface, but in other countries, this might be reduced to 30 percent or less. The Maori and the Balinese also kept surfaces busy, while, as we have seen, the Seri Indians of Tiburón carve a profile of the subject and rely on the inherent beauty of the wood and a relatively high polish to create the desired effect.

Throughout the world of carving, there have always been these variations in amount of detail in form and finish, in coloring, polishing, toning, mounting. A common present-day question is whether or not carved figures, particularly in soft woods, should be painted, and if so, to what degree. Exhibitions differentiate between painted and unpainted figures, and in decoy shows the pieces are as much paintings as they are carvings. But this was also true in Egypt and Greece, where most carvings, even in stone, were painted originally. In Indonesia, statues have been provided with seasonal or festival costumes which are changed regularly, and some of the ancients in Europe did the same thing. In many countries, careful carving of a surface was followed by lacquering in color to make the surface smooth again. Thus precedents can be found for whatever any particular carver decides to do; the weight, if anywhere, being on the side of coloring. Only in sculpture has color been banned in favor of the natural texture of the wood—and even there the surface may be textured in areas, and inconspicuous and artful tinting may be done.

Thus it is difficult to lay down rules about amount of modelling or detail, texturing and finishing. Authorities disagree at every level, as do artists and clients. It eventually becomes a matter of what the individual likes, as it always has been, plus the dictates of fashion, local or worldwide.

Actually, the density, grain, color and other characteristics of the wood; the subject and proposed treatment; the skill of the carver and the eventual disposition of the piece must all be considered from the beginning if a happy marriage of modelling, texture and finish is to be attained. If the wood has a strong figure and dense structure, it will combat any texturing or coloring, unless the coloring is opaque.

As mentioned earlier, many people once thought teak is black, because the Chinese, in particular, lacquered it to destroy the grain, and possibly to suggest ebony. Grain may also distort modelling lines and even a silhouette. I once carved an Arab stallion head in mahogany in which the grain enhanced the arch of the neck, and shortly thereafter a madonna in pine who wore a perpetual grin because of a grain line passing through the modelled mouth. (She *had* to be tinted.)

Similarly, texturing can overpower the basic design or enhance it, depending upon how it is done. The very rough coat of a bear can be simulated either with flat planes or with veiner lines, but some of the most dramatic bears I've seen are smooth and finished with a low gloss. The best decoys have exact feathering carved and painted and veined with a pyrographic needle, but most bird sculptures show no texture whatsoever and avoid the problems of eyes (glass inserts in decoys) and legs—usually metal in painted birds—by not showing either at all. The emphasis in one case is realism, in the other it is suggestion. Take your pick.

My tendency, as a mechanic and engineer, is to over-detail, to blur the profile and surface by excessive modelling and texturing. Other carvers I know are too dependent upon files, rasps and sandpaper, or upon single-coat gloss finishes reminiscent of cabinet-making. Their efforts are directed toward obtaining precision—one mark of a good piece of furniture—and art, strength and individuality may be sacrificed in the process. (I am not making a case for the slapdash wood butcher, but simply warning that exactness can be overdone.)

Sometimes, other considerations are influences. When I decided to place a heroic cardinal atop my "bug tree"—a 12-ft (4 m) surface-carved obelisk—I flew in the face of fact, for cardinals eat seeds rather than insects. Also I caricatured the cardinal, made him unduly fat although the low-relief bugs on the tree were executed in considerable detail. But I could not escape the fact that the cardinal was exposed to wind and weather, therefore had to be finished with marine varnish, which gave him a high gloss. Further, there was no reason to carve feathering; it couldn't be seen from the ground anyway, and any texturing simply increased the points of entry for water and real-life bugs fond of cherry wood.

There is little point in putting a great deal of detail into a carving that will be displayed some distance from the viewer, even though detail is easier as the piece becomes larger. There is no point in carving detail and deep modelling into wood that is too soft or too inclined to split, then have to support it. If the wood is still green or its moisture content is likely to change for any reason after completion, checking will be encouraged by cut lines, and the finish will not stop it. If a piece is likely to be handled, details and weak areas are likely to be damaged; and if the wood is light-colored, they will certainly pick up soiling. On the other hand, a table top to be covered by glass can be quite intricate, because it is likely to be inspected at close range. A carving to serve as a screen is a natural subject for openwork (piercing), and the openwork may actually help reduce the tendency to warp by equalizing humidity rapidly on the two faces. The Javanese recognized these things in making moldings and other decorations for open-air shrines; they are usually pierced carvings, (as the example shows.) The openwork in the Javanese panels shown here serves yet another purpose; it gives the composition an airy quality and enables it to benefit from a suitable texture or color on the wall behind it.

Sometimes, detailed modelling is necessary to a design, as in the Celtic bird brooch, where the various levels are separated by texturing and modelling, and important elements are emphasized—in this case by textural lack. Incidentally, this particular design emphasizes another point: You don't have to stick to the letter of the original design if you are changing medium. The original was a small cast-brass brooch; mine was a 6-in (15 cm) bird carved in low relief on vermilion wood, where it was the subject of view, not primarily a decoration. So I intensified some elements. Also, vermilion takes a high polish from the cutting tool, so some texturing and modelling was necessary to make the carving stand out. I could, of course, have sanded the whole thing and blurred the lines.

Contrast the Celtic bird with the animal panels on page 102. These are obviously adapted to incising—mere carving of the outlines on a flat sur-face—or to shallow bosting and roughing of the background, so the elements stand out. Wavy lines under some of the animals could be incised in either case, and color could be used or the background roughened to increase the contrast.

BULLOCK CART Java 3/4" yellowish wood

Both Balinese & Javanese carve pierced panels, but Balinese usually choose religious or mythical subjects, Javanese choose domestic ones.

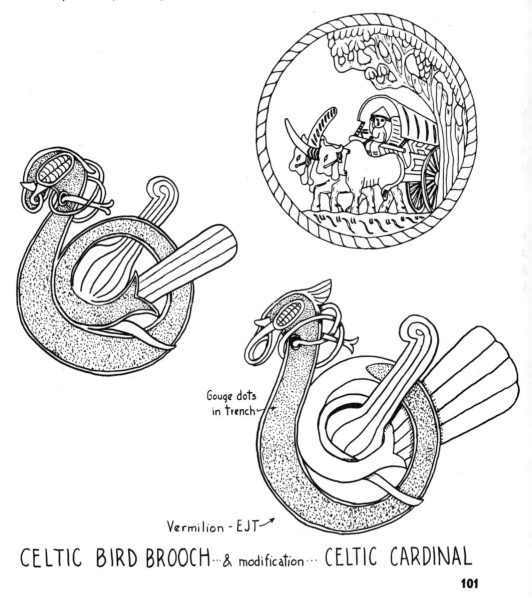

Gouge dots in trench →

Vermilion - EJT →

CELTIC BIRD BROOCH ... & modification ... CELTIC CARDINAL

101

ANIMAL PANELS
Shower-curtain designs in Chiapas, Mex.

Note that the veiner, which makes these fine lines, is an essential adjunct to either knife or chisels. In fact, these designs offer so many possibilities in interpretation that I copied them from a shower curtain in Mexico—and haven't attempted to carve them as yet. The panels and the cardinal, incidentally, provide an answer to that perennial question of tyro carvers, "Where can I get new ideas?"

Another example of careful use of texturing to obtain a pleasing effect is the owl from Bali. It is, of course, a stylized owl, so its feathers are stylized outlines. The "rays" around the eyes are used to add emphasis to the eyes and bill as well as to give the "ears" shape. However, a large part of the body is unmarked except for occasional pairs of veiner lines to emphasize the curvature. The boar contrasts with it in that it is much more true to life; it has wrinkles and bends and even some white lines painted on it for wrinkles, a seemingly unnecessary addition as far as I am concerned.

Modelling is obviously necessary for the cow and dog skeletons—which aren't skeletons at all in reality. The ridges in spine and ribs and the slots in legs suggest a skeleton, which is belied by the complete head. These two, by the way, were made by Indians in the village of San Martín Tilcajete, Oaxaca, Mexico, who are primarily farmers and adobe makers. These Indians have

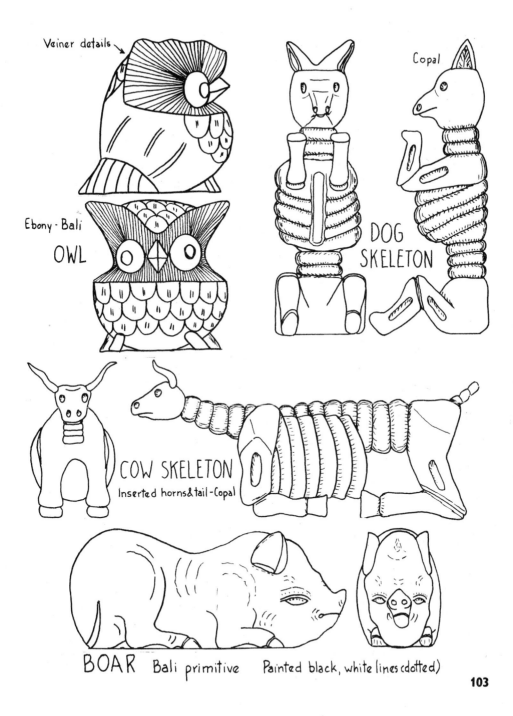

Veiner details

Copal

Ebony - Bali
OWL

DOG
SKELETON

COW SKELETON
Inserted horns & tail - Copal

BOAR Bali primitive   Painted black, white lines (dotted)

become well known, however, for their carvings of similarly designed human skeletons, popular in Mexico to celebrate the Day of the Dead, November 1. Painting such figures would be rather absurd, even though they are carved in copal, a soft and very white wood.

A stylization somewhat akin to these is the armadillo, from the same town. Here the carver used knife cross-hatching to suggest the scaly coat of the animal, but again used no color. A very elaborate and imaginative sculpture from this town is the two-headed monkey, which is about 10 in (25 cm) high. I am at a total loss to explain the symbolism, and the carver had nothing to say; he felt it was strong enough to live without explanations. Strangely, he provided scales on the monkey body with random criss-cross lines, as well as on the bell of the trumpet-shaped object the monkey is holding, and drilled holes at the base of the dog head and slots in the bell of the trumpet. The result is a conversation piece, if nothing more—and one that was snapped up by a Mexico City collector.

Some carvings almost cry out for strong lines and color. Examples are the ceremonial drums from the South Pacific. The carving is simple and strong, and only resembles people by coincidence. Actually, these faces represent spirits, and are highly colored in consequence.

Another example of this is the little fish from Guerrero, Mexico. It is decorated with gouge cuts, but also has stylized color to suggest the trout that inspired it.

The ultimate in present-day stylizing and use of color is the bebek, or dragon duck, from Bali, a ritual object carved with a hidden compartment in its back for prayers to the gods. It is made in parts and carved in very great detail, then highly colored and gilded. There is no likelihood that it will not be noticed regardless of location, because the original is life-size! Designed for religious purposes, it has become a spot of color in American and other homes far from Bali, largely because it contrasts in boldness with most moderate present-day decoration. It also contrasts sharply with most modern Balinese figure carving, which relies on flowing lines for its effects.

To sum up: There are *no* rigid conventions about modelling and texturing. It appears to be more acceptable, however, to use both in moderation, particularly on small carvings. Remember always that texturing tends to subdue, rather than accentuate, a surface. Color is usually best as thin tints which are more suggestive of the color than realistic and show the wood beneath. Further,

STYLIZED ARMADILLO
Oaxaca. Copal, with knife grooving

← Gouge cuts

FISH - Guerrero, Mex.

By Agostino Cruz, in copal

2-HEADED MONKEY
Body has "scales"

Serpent

CEREMONIAL DRUMS
S. Pacific (Hollowed logs)

color is in most cases effective primarily on soft and colorless woods with no decided grain, or where it is necessary to overcome the effect of grain, or if the fact that it is a carving rather than a molding or a cast form is unimportant. The possibilities of silhouette shape and pierced carving on flat-panel design should not be neglected. Beautiful hardwoods should be permitted to be themselves unless the carved object must serve some utilitarian purpose. Finishes usually are better if a low gloss is obtained rather than a high one, and carved surfaces should not be sanded before finishing unless the risk to carved lines is justified; it should then be done with care. Finally, and perhaps most important, all of the factors of modelling, texturing and finishing should be kept in mind when the design is selected or created.

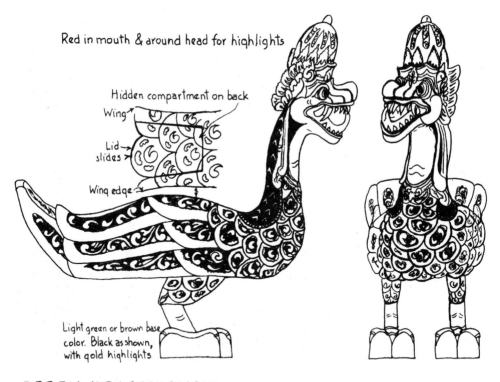

Red in mouth & around head for highlights

Hidden compartment on back

Wing

Lid slides

Wing edge

Light green or brown base color. Black as shown, with gold highlights

BEBEK (DRAGON DUCK) Bali Painted

CHAPTER XIX

You Can Whittle Ivory

That is, if you can find it

MAN HAS REVERED IVORY as a symbol of opulence, purity and innocence since some time in the Paleolithic Era, over 15,000 years ago. He had mastodon, mammoth, elephant, rhino, hippo and walrus tusks, and whale teeth as sources, so wherever man was, there were carved objects of ivory.

Ivory is still perhaps the finest carving material for miniatures, but it is unlikely to remain that much longer, for now all of its sources are numbered among the endangered species. Eskimos and Indians of the Northwest Coast can still get walrus ivory, northern peoples still dig up mammoth and mastodon tusks in Asia, Europe and North America, and some carvers still have private sources in Africa. But most of us must depend upon "old" ivory: pool balls, walrus tusks, big scrimshawed pieces, and the like. For others, bone and deerhorn are the alternates.

The Egyptians were carving ivory into elaborate figures, and the Chinese were making it into intricate pierced panels well over 5,000 years ago. The Phoenicians had a thriving industry; Greece, Rome, Byzantium, the Moslem countries, India, Burma, Indonesia, Japan and the Eskimos have carved ivory over succeeding millennia. Sailors of many countries perpetuated the Eskimo art of "scrimshaw"—scratching the dentine layer of walrus ivory or whale teeth and filling the scratches with India ink or colored pigment—and it is still a popular occupation. But the real art of carving ivory is relatively rare these days, except in China, India and among the Eskimos. Germany, the USSR and Japan still have pockets of ivory carvers, much of this being mastodon or mammoth ivory. In the Azores, Chile and other whaling areas, carvers have turned to whale and shark teeth; in other areas boar tusks, deer horns and bone are the materials.

My own interest in ivory has developed over a long period. I bought occasional pieces when I could afford them as long as 40 years ago. They were mainly Chinese, but I have Russian, German, Portuguese, Indian, Japanese and Hong Kong examples. I whacked out occasional inlay and other pieces from carefully hoarded piano keys, watched scrimshaw carvers at work as far away as Hong Kong, and as near as Long Island, even tried to buy the tools from a Chinese in Hong Kong. Several years ago, a friend gave me two 10-year-old walrus tusks, so I've made over a dozen pieces of my own recently, using a pocketknife, small woodcarving chisels, coping saw and rasps. So ivory can be carved by hand, although the more prolific Germans and even Eskimos I've seen carving it in recent years were using power tools.

All ivory is essentially like your own teeth. It has an outer layer of very hard enamel, then a much thicker layer of dentine, and finally a core of much softer material that looks like slightly discolored clotted cheese pressed solid. Usual practice is to chip or grind off the enamel, both to remove surface defects and discoloration and to expose the softer and whiter dentine. This is not necessary, however—witness on pgs. 109–110 the low-relief animal poses I carved in the enamel layer. Enamel is harder to carve than dentine, but a design of any depth goes through it anyway.

Ivory has so little grain that this is unimportant. It has very little tendency to split, although old ivory does tend to separate in layers as it dries out. Thus, for example, my carvings of the polar bear and puffins are mounted on the butts of walrus tusks; partially separated portions of the dentine layer I sawed through and split off. On a conventional walrus tusk, the dentine layer will be perhaps $\frac{3}{8}$ in (9.5 mm) thick at the base and go clear through near the tip, so pieces like the Billikens can be made from it. Larger pieces, like the walrus, are carved of cross-slices, so will include some of the core material. This is slightly yellow, with a honeycomb or pebbly pattern, because that's where the blood vessels and nerves were. (The polar bear is mounted on the jaw end of such core material, which is quite dark there.)

Elephant ivory also tends to separate as it grows older, just as some woods do, particularly if the carving is kept in a thoroughly dry place. Large blocks of elephant ivory are sensitive to sudden heat changes. A high-intensity lamp too close to the block, too much concentration with a power burr or a grinder, or even sudden change from a cool storage room to a warm room may cause cracking. (Also, carving ivory with power tools may cause burning, and is likely to cause a smell like that of old bones burning.)

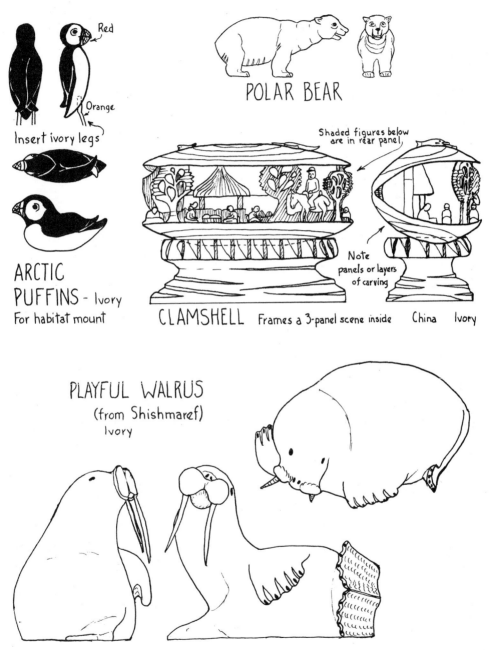

Red

Orange

Insert ivory legs

POLAR BEAR

Shaded figures below
are in rear panel.

ARCTIC
PUFFINS - Ivory
For habitat mount

CLAMSHELL   Frames a 3-panel scene inside   China   Ivory

Note
panels or layers
of carving

PLAYFUL WALRUS
(from Shishmaref)
Ivory

109

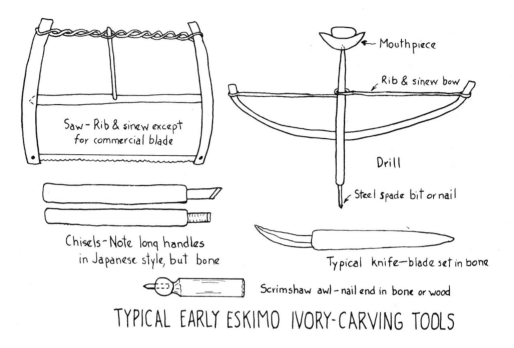

Saw – Rib & sinew except
for commercial blade

Mouthpiece

Rib & sinew bow

Drill

Steel spade bit or nail

Chisels–Note long handles
in Japanese style, but bone

Typical knife—blade set in bone

Scrimshaw awl – nail end in bone or wood

TYPICAL EARLY ESKIMO IVORY-CARVING TOOLS

Because ivory is so hard and strong, it is possible to carve a great deal of detail into it and to achieve lacy pierced carvings. The Chinese have always surpassed at this—note the examples sketched. It is also possible to make very small carvings from chips; I have an ivory camel going through the eye of a darning needle, and a red seed about $\frac{3}{8}$ in (9.5 mm) in diameter that contains a hundred mixed animals of ivory, mainly camels and elephants. Both are Indian in origin, and made some years back.

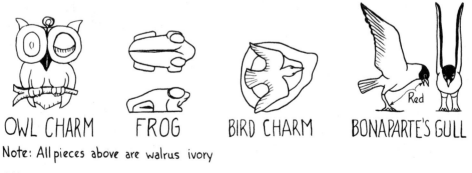

OWL CHARM   FROG   BIRD CHARM   BONAPARTE'S GULL

Red

Note: All pieces above are walrus ivory

110

The usual way to work ivory is to saw a blank, then to shape it as much as possible with drills, files and sanding sticks. But surface designs must be put in with an edged tool. For lines, an engraver's burin will work, as well as a V-tool or veiner if the piece can be securely held. (If the tool slips, you'll find that your hand is much softer than ivory.) A hand vise or a sandbag may be helpful, depending upon shape. But I find a pocketknife works very well, or a hook blade such as is used for leather. The included angle of the edge should be increased, however; sharpening must be frequent. Even then, chips are appallingly small.

Polishing must be done very carefully to avoid scratching and dulling the surface as well as blurring sharp edges. Ivory is such an intense white that blurred edges tend to disappear, leaving nothing visible but an amorphous blob. Very fine sandpaper or emery paper, preferably worn, can be used for rough smoothing, but for finishing, something like jeweler's rouge and a cloth is better. The final polishing, at least among the Eskimos, is with paste silver polish.

After polishing, you will probably find that your carved lines are not visible at a short distance. The Japanese and Chinese speed up the normal antiquing process (deposition of dirt in crevices) by coating the carving with strong tea or bathing it in smoke, then wiping it off. A light-colored wood stain will do the same thing, but be sure to work only small areas and wipe off the surface fast! This leaves darker tones in the crevices. It is also possible to draw in lines with India ink or to fill grooves with ink or pigment. This has a tendency, however, to give the carving a harsh look. A lighter-colored ink of the transparent kind will work better to define detail carving or important lines, but even this must be used with care. In scrimshaw, of course, which is really a form of etching, the technique was to smoke or otherwise darken the surface, then scratch the design in with a knife point, sharpened nail or awl, fill in with ink, then sand or scrape off the surface discoloration, leaving the lines filled. This is possible because ivory does not absorb the ink, as wood would, so it has no tendency to blur or spread. But beware the mistaken line! The ink will reveal *all* lines and depressions.

Eskimos carved bone and soapstone (a soft variety called greenstone), whalebone and even jade, providing their tools would cut them. They used such exotic equipment as sharkskin for sanding, and bow drills backed by jaw pressure. Typical tools are sketched.

CHAPTER XX

Bone, Stone, Shell and Nuts

Wood is not the only carving material

ONCE POSSESSED OF TOOLS, man carved anything that came to hand, from stone and shell to bone, horn, nuts and bark. Wood was plentiful and more generally useful as well as more amenable to tools, that's all. In Africa, India and parts of Europe, they carved shell, and still do. Pioneers here carved peach stones, cherry pits and other nuts, and still do. The same may be said for coconuts and gourds.

The principal problem with most of these materials is that they are harder and more brittle than wood, so tools must have a greater included angle and be sharpened more frequently. Files, rasps, abrasives, saws and drills are much more often necessary, and modern rotary tools like hand grinders and flexible-shaft tools are much faster. The bone carvings pictured here were done with a flexible-shaft tool.

Ruth T. Brunstetter of Hyde Park, New York, is a painter, art instructor and show judge noted particularly for her scenes of nature. She has illustrated several books, including a recent one of trees of North America. Recently, she became interested in animal skeletons and taught herself processes for cleaning, bleaching and preserving bones, then mounting and articulating them. She now has more than 50 skeletons, ranging from a mouse to a 10-ft (3 m) alligator and a buffalo, including most of the animals of her native state, as well as a wallaby and a barracuda. They fill her house when they aren't on exhibit, and she lectures on them in many places, including the Smithsonian.

This hobby led Mrs. Brunstetter into power carving of bones, usually buffalo, which she gets from a neighbor who has a small buffalo herd. Now her carvings are being exhibited and sold.

Eskimos carve whalebone upon occasion, and various kinds of stone,

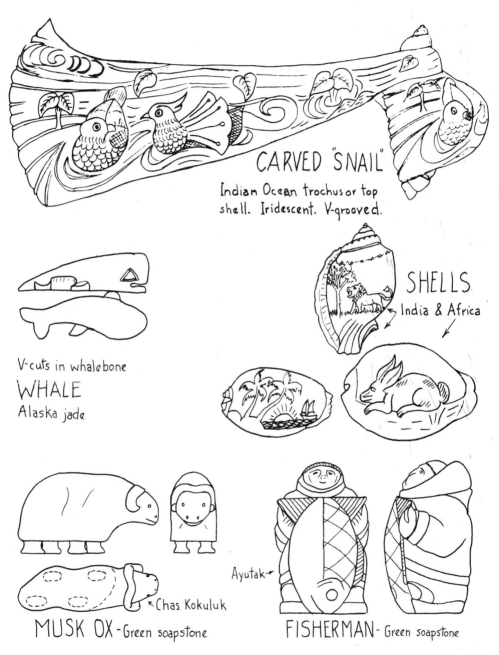

CARVED "SNAIL"

Indian Ocean trochus or top shell. Iridescent. V-grooved.

SHELLS
India & Africa

V-cuts in whalebone
WHALE
Alaska jade

Ayutak →

← Chas. Kokuluk

MUSK OX – Green soapstone

FISHERMAN – Green soapstone

113

principally greenstone, a form of soapstone (on the East Coast, gray soapstone was more common), and Alaskan jade. Whalebone and soapstone can be whittled easily, but tend to be brittle. The Northwest Coast Indians carved and formed mountain-sheep horn, as do Chilean Indians, Indonesians and Russian peasants. This material is soft, and tends to "stick" when cut. Coastal people of India, Africa, and the Americas have all carved shell, as well as using pieces of it as inlays in wood carvings; one tribe in Mexico even makes mosaics by careful placing of abalone shell in a pitch base. The composition is inlaid in wood and may be a cross, or even a miniature violin or guitar.

My intent in mentioning all these materials is merely to suggest options. Ruth Brunstetter began working with skeletons to relax from painting and housework and now has taken up bone carving as a further means of relaxation. I've found that the challenge of carving ivory and bone is quite different from that of carving wood. Perhaps you will as well.

(*Above*) *This fishpin, an example of power carving of buffalo bones, is by Ruth Brunstetter. Shaping is somewhat restricted by cutters available, but the material takes well to polishing.*

(*Below*) *Greenstone, a form of soapstone and relatively soft, is found in Alaska and has been worked there by both Eskimos and Indians. The musk ox at the right and the bear at the left are probably handmade, but the Eskimo with a fish in the middle is probably a product of a "factory" in Seattle, which imports the stone and exports "native art" for tourists in Alaska.*

CHAPTER XXI

Make Your Own D-Adzes

The favorite tool of the Northwest Coast Indians

CARVERS IN EGYPT, almost 5,000 years ago, as shown in an ancient wall decoration on the next page (courtesy The Metropolitan Museum of Art, New York) were already using the chisel, mallet and adz. The mallet was like a small bat, and the pounding surface was the butt of the handle, or the chisel was used alone if the wood was soft enough to permit it. What is most interesting, however, is the use of the adz, which is relatively unknown to most American carvers.

In various forms (see sketches), the adz was the basic woodcarving tool, not only of the Egyptians, but also of the Africans, American West Coast Indians, Eskimos, Polynesians and New Guinea carvers, among others. It is also familiar among Italians, but not among the Germans and English. Some years ago, when I attempted to buy an adz for demonstration purposes, the suppliers in New York were out of stock (although several forms of the tool were shown in their catalogs) and unworried about it, because their specialists felt that the adz was much too dangerous a tool for "amateurs."

Early adzes had heads of the hardest stone available, and it should be pointed out that they had many applications other than carving wood. They were also used for tilling the ground and for squaring timbers; the former need disappeared with the development of the plow and the latter with the ready availability of planed lumber. When bronze, and then steel, became available for blades, the adz became a much more productive tool, although it should be pointed out that even in the early days, work with the adz was often primarily the removal of charcoal—the interior shape of a canoe, for example, was roughed out by burning. Some adzes had interchangeable blades, others were double-bladed. John E. Hendricks (whose Indian name is Wahnadagee) of

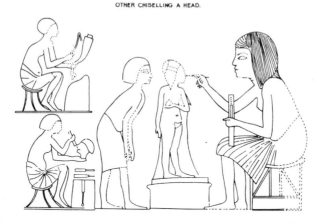

FROM WALL-PAINTING IN THE TOMB OF HUYA AT TELL EL AMARNA.   DYN. XVIII (ABOUT 1375 B.C.)

Bellingham, Washington, wrote to explain to me the making and use of the modern D-adz, one of several shapes still in use by carvers in his area. His discussion led me to make a couple of D-adzes, which I have found to be excellent tools, easy to control and rapid in chip removal. The American Northwest Coast and Arctic Indians use them for carving totem poles, bowls, spoons, ladles and the like. They also use the elbow-type (regular) adz as well, but the D-adz has been the favorite for many years because it is easier to master and control. Blades are made from old mill files and rasps, smaller sizes from 6-in (15 cm) files and larger ones from 10-in (25 cm) and 12-in (30 cm) files. But let Wahnadagee tell the story:

"Handles can be plain, or quite ornamental, as show in the sketches, and should be made of a hard, shock-resisting wood like rock maple. A channel is cut on the striking face (the vertical bar of the D) to fit the blade, a section of old mill file or rasp—for smaller adzes from 6-in files and larger ones from 10- or 12-in ones. The file is bolted in so it has light bearing at the bottom towards the direction of impact. Such a tool just can't be beat for totem carving or milling and sculpting of cedar wood in general. With a little practice, it can do all the shaping of something even as small as a spoon up to the point of final detail. I have one that is metal except for the grip and is a real work-horse.

While I use a hand axe for some roughing, I prefer the D-adz because you

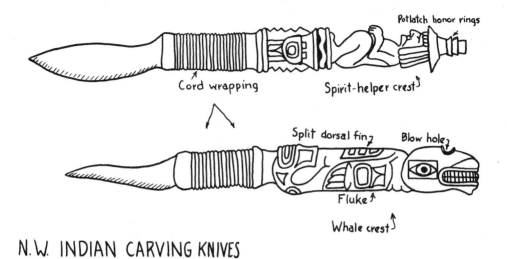

Potlatch honor rings

Cord wrapping

Spirit-helper crest⌐

Split dorsal fin⌐　Blow hole⌐

Fluke ↑

Whale crest⌐

N.W. INDIAN CARVING KNIVES

face the surface you're working on, rather than viewing it from one side. Also, I've always made my own tools, many of them from old saw steel. I now have many tools, but I still prefer the old ones, as well as the old ways for curing and preparing native woods such as cedar. (I make sewn-leather sheaths for all cutting edges for the sake of safety as well as for edge preservation.)

D-adzes are easy to make to suit the user. The only question that may trouble some makers is how to drill holes in a file or rasp. I have two methods: On small files, I put a plumber's-torch flame on the exact spot to be drilled, and hold it there until the spot turns bright red—about 30 seconds. Then I let it cool in air (don't quench it in water or you'll harden it again). It will then be soft enough to drill with HSS bits. If the file is smaller, or a fragment for a knife or firmer, I wrap a wet cloth around the knife end before heating. [A setup for controlling annealing is sketched—Author.]

I anneal larger files or rasps in my trash-burner stove, putting the piece to be annealed on top of the ashes and building my regular morning woodfire on top of it. I take the annealed piece out the next morning before I re-start the fire, and drill as before. This is followed by grinding off the serrations or file pattern, and cutting the blade to desired length.

The temper is tested with a file at the cutting edge; it should file about like a good axe does. One doesn't want a flint-hard edge, which is likely to shatter

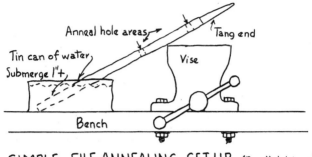

SIMPLE FILE-ANNEALING SET-UP (Roy Hutchings)

or break off. If the blade is too soft, it can be re-tempered before sharpening. I do that, on the few occasions when it is necessary, with the plumber's torch, heating the cutting edge until it is bright red and quenching in bear's grease or old cylinder oil. (If old cylinder oil is used—which is more readily available than bear grease for most of us—be sure it is free of gasoline by pretesting a small quantity of it for flare-up.) Actually, in this case, the blade is slightly case-hardened.

Some tribes do not bolt the blade, but bind it on as on the knife pictured. This is somewhat harder to do than bolting, and in my opinion not worth the trouble. It is also possible to install a screw-clamp arrangement, but that is usually bulky and clumsy. With the bolt method, the holes in file and handle can be matched, and the only problem is some wear on bolt holes after a lot of hard use. By the way, the bolts should be of the countersunk type, so they don't project from the face of the blade.

I make blades for carving knives from worn-out carpenter's handsaws, particularly Craftsman® (Sears) or Disston® brands. To use such steel, remove the handle, then clamp the blade in a wide-jaw machinist's vise so about a $\frac{3}{4}$-in (19 mm) width of the blade is between the jaws. Start at the front or outer end of the saw. Now, beat along the blade at the top of the vise with a heavy ballpein hammer. This will start a break along the vise line. Move the saw along a vise width and reclamp, then hammer it to continue the crack. The resulting strip can be ground or broken into desired lengths and shaped by grinding. The toothed-edge strip, by the way can be made into short saws for rough-shaping soapstone (steatite), bone or other carving materials. The steel can also be formed into so-called "crooked knives" by beating a section carefully on and over an iron rod, pipe or mandrel.

118

To secure a blade into the handle, grind a slot in the handle end, then put epoxy glue (I use Elmer's®) into that slot and the slot sawed in the handle, assemble in position, and bind temporarily with cord. When the glue has set, replace the cord with a rawhide, bearhide, or fishline wrapping. Coat the wrapping with a mixture of two-thirds spar varnish and one-third turpentine or equivalent. This preservative prevents fraying or chafing. (In the old days, the preservative was a special pitch.) I prefer to sharpen such blades from one side only; this lengthens edge life and the tool cuts more like a draw-shave.

The beads and colors on knives and adzes have definite traditional meanings. Black is the decorative color for tools, which are not ceremonial. Ceremonial colors are related to the spirit language. Red denotes blood, the life giver for animals and fish. Blue denotes the Great Spirit and the Sky People, the Thunderbird's house and other spiritual things. Dark blue denotes bravery and courage; the voice of horror is in its tone. Green, yellow and brown honor our Mother the Earth; they suggest gracious giving to sustain life and the rhythm and beauty of growing things. They suggest annual renewal, the chain of life."

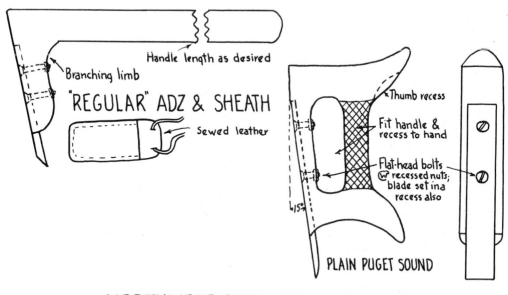

Handle length as desired

Branching limb

"REGULAR" ADZ & SHEATH

Sewed leather

Thumb recess

Fit handle & recess to hand

Flat-head bolts (w/ recessed nuts; blade set in a recess also

PLAIN PUGET SOUND

NORTHWEST COAST INDIAN D-ADZES

Sharpening, Fitting Drawing to Wood, and Finishing

How do you sharpen tools?

THE EDGE OF A TOOL—any tool—is really like a saw under the microscope, with teeth projecting at various angles and feathery filaments projecting from them. The sharper the edge, the fewer the feathers and the smaller and better-aligned the teeth. Using the edge misaligns the teeth and blunts them, so constant, and to me boring, resharpening is necessary.

There are four steps to sharpening: grinding, whetting, honing and stropping. Grinding is the first and coarsest step and is rarely necessary, except on tools that have been nicked or broken or resharpened so often that the edge is blunt. Grinding was once done on a grindstone, which moved at slow speed, but is now done on a high-speed wheel, so the danger of burning the tool edge is ever-present. If the wheel surface is loaded—filled with grains of soft metal or wood or even pencil lead—or the tool edge is not kept cool, there is danger of burning the thin edge. This draws the temper, evidenced by blue, brown or purple discoloration, and makes the metal soft so it will not hold an edge. Thus, you should never grind a tool unless it is absolutely essential and unless you know how, and then you should cool the tip twice as often as you consider necessary.

The next two operations, whetting and honing, are also grinding operations, but with progressively finer-grained stones. They are usually done by hand. Whetting is done on Washita, a yellowish or grayish natural stone, honing on Arkansas, a white, very hard, uniform and fine-grained white stone. Arkansas is also the material for "slips," the small shaped stones for taking the feather edge off the inside of gouges and V-tools, as mentioned later. There are now manufactured stones for doing both of these operations, often with one side for whetting, the other honing. In day-to-day carving, honing is frequent, whetting much less so unless the wood being carved is particularly hard or abrasive.

The final operation is stropping, which is what a barber does to a straight razor. It is essentially stroking the edge on leather to align the tiny teeth, and produces an ultra-sharp edge like that of a razor.

The typical tool nowadays is sold ground and whetted. It is quite sharp to the touch, but requires honing and stropping before using, if you are particular. Knives are ground so the blade itself has the proper included angle, about 15°, and require only "touch-up" for sharpening. A properly ground firmer has an included angle of about 30°, 15° each side of center, and the center line of the tip should be that of the tool also. Gouges have the same included angle, but it is all ground on the outside of the tool—the concave inner surface should be flat, and left that way.

Some carvers prefer a hollow-ground edge, one that is slightly concave, usually from the peripheral shape of the wheel which grinds them. (The hollow-ground shape is exaggerated in a straight razor.) Hollow grinding makes initial whetting and honing easier because the angle just behind the cutting edge is less than it should be, reducing drag behind the cutting edge, and is claimed to make the tool stay sharp longer. This is true in cutting soft woods, but may make the edge turn or nick on hard ones or imperfections.

I have tried to sketch the motions used in sharpening tools, both to maintain their edges and to insure uniform wear on the stone. Many stones become channelled through excessive wear in the middle, and this results in dullness in the center of a firmer cutting edge and rounding of the outer corners. (All operations on stones are done by pushing the edge toward the wheel or stone, while honing is done by passing the heel over the strop first.) The stone should be kept lubricated with thin machine oil, or even a 50-50 mixture of machine oil and kerosene, and should be wiped off and replaced when it turns gray from included metal particles. Periodically also, the stone should be washed with benzine or gasoline, or boiled in water containing a little soda. This lifts out soaked-in oil and grit. If you have manufactured stones, just heat them in an oven and wipe them off; the heating causes the oil to exude and lift the grit with it.

To sharpen a knife, I use a rotary or figure-8 motion (A), bearing down a bit harder as the edge is moving forward and lifting the handle a bit part of the

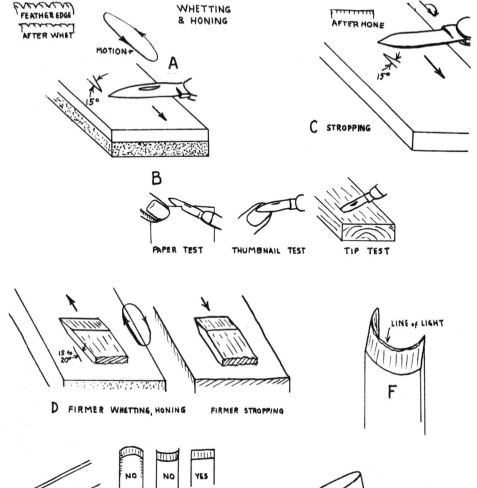

FEATHER EDGE

AFTER WHET

WHETTING & HONING

MOTION

A

15°

AFTER HONE

15°

C STROPPING

B

PAPER TEST   THUMBNAIL TEST   TIP TEST

LINE of LIGHT

15 to 20°

D FIRMER WHETTING, HONING   FIRMER STROPPING

F

NO   NO   YES

KEEP TOOLS SQUARE

INNER BEVEL

G

E

WHETTING, HONING & STROPPING A GOUGE

HONING INNER BEVEL IN GOUGE

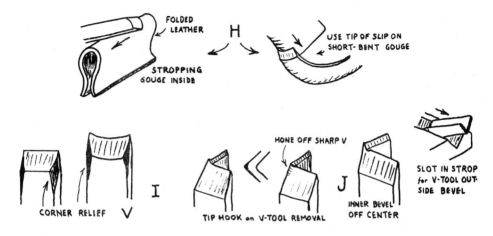

FOLDED LEATHER

H

USE TIP OF SLIP ON SHORT-BENT GOUGE

STROPPING GOUGE INSIDE

CORNER RELIEF

I

V

HONE OFF SHARP V

TIP HOOK on V-TOOL REMOVAL

INNER BEVEL OFF CENTER

J

SLOT IN STROP for V-TOOL OUTSIDE BEVEL

time to be sure I touch up the tip, which takes most wear. Unless the knife is very dull, a few swirls on whetstone and hone in turn should do it. Sharpness can be tested by trying the edge on a fingernail or on paper—it should "stick" on the former and slice the latter when drawn across (B). This operation will also detect any nicks or dull areas. Then the knife is drawn for a stroke or two over each side of the strop (C)—which is usually a piece of thin plywood with rough leather glued on one side, smooth on the other. The rough leather is impregnated with oil and crocus powder, while the smooth side has oil alone. Stropping is done with the blade heel-first; you can speed the operation by rolling the blade over the heel at the end of a stroke and reversing direction. Incidentally, it is good practice to learn to strop a tool almost absent-mindedly, so you can do it while you plan the next cut.

Carving tools are sharpened in much the same manner, particularly the firmer (D). However, the sharpening of gouges is a bit more tricky. The tool must be rotated slightly as it passes over the stone, so the entire edge is treated (E), and too much roll means rounded corners while too little means dull corners that will tear the wood rather than cutting it. Dullness in an area may be seen as a line of light (F). Also, because all sharpening is done from one side, a wire edge forms on the inside; it can be felt as a tiny burr with a fingernail. Thus the final operation in honing a gouge is to pass a slip down inside to take off the wire edge, and to do the same thing with a piece of leather in stropping. I have sketched the method (G, H). Some carvers thin the edges of chisels behind the cutting edge to relieve drag (I).

The parting or V-tool is a special problem to sharpen, because there is a tendency for a tit to form at the tip (J), or for the sides to slope back. This must be guarded against at all costs, and it may be advisable to whet or hone away just a very little of the bottom of the V at the tip so the cutting edge there is no thicker than it is at the sides.

This lengthy discussion is really only an introduction to the problem of sharpening tools and keeping them sharp, but it may serve as a warning against idle whacking or mistreatment of a tool during carving. It also explains why so many carvers hate sharpening and try to avoid it by every possible means, including disposable blades. Some of them have worked out methods of re-grinding in fixtures on belt sanders, and whetting and honing in a single operation on buffing wheels, even grinding and whetting gouges on shaped wheels as the manufacturers do. But for most of us, hand methods work best, because the frequency really isn't as great as it seems.

The carver who sharpens his own tools soon learns to treat the edges with care, both when in use and when in storage. Tools should be placed on the bench or workplace side by side, with their sharp ends toward you so you can pick out what you want rapidly and surely. They should be stored in slots so the edges don't touch, and when carried about should be in a portable carrier or in a canvas or other roll that protects the ends. Also, after arrival and before use, it is advisable at least to strop and probably to hone each tool; some professionals I know, like barbers, strop a tool just before they use it each time, and have hone and strop readily available all the time, as much in evidence as the tools they service.

How do you make the drawing fit the wood?

VERY OFTEN, the design you want to use doesn't quite fit the wood, usually because the design is too small. In these mechanized days, it is easy to make direct (same-size) copies, but the old photostat machine, which was capable of enlarging or reducing is not available except in art studios, which also often have photographic enlargers. If you can take, or have taken, a negative of the drawing, you can either have a print made of proper size, or put the negative in an enlarger and sketch the outlines to size, either on a sheet of paper or directly on the wood. For three-dimensional carvings, this is really all you need: a guide to saw away waste wood.

But let's say none of the above is available, and you have a two-view sketch that must be made double size. For a rough shape, the simplest method is to take a rubber band that is a couple of inches longer than the combined width of the wider sketch and the wood on which it is to be traced. (If you haven't one band that long, link several together.) Tie a pencil at one end of the band and make a small loop for a thumbtack at the other. Mark with ink a line one-half the distance from the tack to the pencil. Then Scotch-tape the sketch toward the left edge of a large breadboard or other flat surface that can take a thumbtack. Put the piece of wood beside it on the right. Set the thumbtack into the baseboard at the left, so the ink mark on the band is just short of the closest line on the sketch. Now stretch the band so the ink mark aligns with a point on the sketch, and move the wood blank until the pencil point is on the corresponding point on its surface. Draw on the block with the pencil and stretch the band as you draw to keep the ink line aligned with the lines of the sketch. (This is much more difficult to describe than it is to do.)

For triple size, the ink mark should be at one-third the distance from tack to pencil, and so on. For any enlargement, in fact, all you need is the ratio. Thus for $1\frac{1}{2}$ scale, divide the rubber-band length by 3 and put the ink mark at 2; for $2\frac{1}{4}$ scale, divide the band length by $4\frac{1}{2}$ and put the ink mark at 2. This method is in fact a crude pantograph, which most of us do not have.

The traditional method of enlarging is by the method of squares. Draw a grid of $\frac{1}{8}$-in (3.2 mm) squares on transparent paper, larger than the original sketch you have. Draw a similar grid on the wood blank or on a plain sheet of paper, but make the squares as much larger as you need, that is, for double size use $\frac{1}{4}$-in (6.4 mm) squares, for triple size $\frac{3}{8}$-in (9.6 mm) squares. Now lay the transparent grid over the sketch and copy the design on the block square by square. Save the grid, by the way; it can be used over and over—even on good silhouette photographs of a subject—and is particularly useful in laying out relief carvings, where precise outlines are necessary.

Another method is one I use quite frequently in laying out sketches from a photograph. Make a right-angle template of paper or plastic big enough so the arms extend to the width and height of the part of the photo you wish to copy. Set this over the photo so one arm is the base and the other just touches the leftmost element of the design, and hold it there with tape. Now prominent points can be located by measuring from the base and the side. If you lay out a similar right angle on the sketch pad, the points can be located one by one.

3 WAYS TO CHANGE SIZE

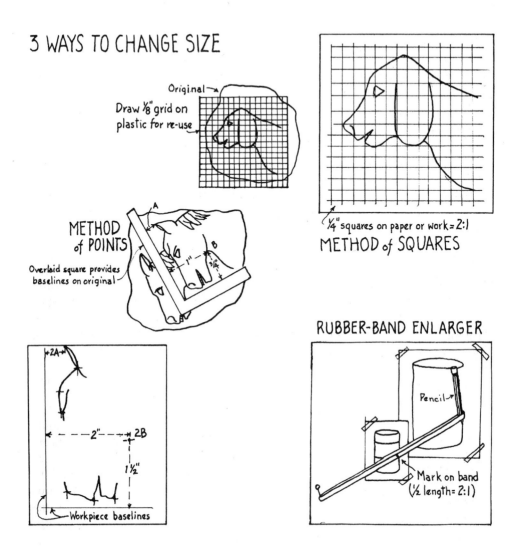

Original →

Draw ⅛" grid on plastic for re-use

¼" squares on paper or work = 2:1

METHOD of SQUARES

METHOD of POINTS

Overlaid square provides baselines on original

RUBBER-BAND ENLARGER

Pencil →

Mark on band (½ length = 2:1)

←2A→

2" ·· ≈ 2B

1½"

Workpiece baselines

Each measurement must of course be multiplied (or divided, if you are reducing) by the ratio of the size of the original to the copy, that is, twice for double size, and so on. This is slow, but very accurate, and suitable for complex designs. The sketch is of course made by drawing suitable-shape lines between the points. The number of points necessary is a function of the complexity of the design and your own skill at drawing.

How shall you finish your carvings?

FINISHING is so much a matter of the individual carving and of personal preference that it is difficult to lay down even general rules. Thus I have indicated all through this book what finish is used, as far as I can determine if I did not make the piece myself.

If a piece is made in soft wood and painted, I prefer to see the color put on thinly and wiped down somewhat, so the wood shows through in flat areas while the color accents lines and depressions. To prevent color from soaking in and over-coloring cross-grain areas, I flat-spray varnish first. Then I use oil pigments thinned with flat varnish or drier, but acrylics can be thinned and used the same way. Heavy painting creates a shiny, plastic effect and denies the hand work and the wood.

It is also possible to dye or stain soft-wood pieces; I have done both with pleasing results. I recently dyed the small birds of a mobile with cloth dyes in the absence of anything else; the colors were vivid at least. I also have a series of German sal-ammoniac-based stains called "Beiz," developed particularly for wood. These include wax, so color and polish are applied in a single operation, as with some American oil-and-wax stains. With the latter, and contrary to instructions on the can, it is usually preferable to give the piece a coat or two of flat (satin) spray varnish before staining; this prevents the stain from over-soaking in end grain and causing over-emphasis there.

For hardwood carvings, I prefer not to use fillers or much of the other paraphernalia and procedure of cabinetmaking—unless the carving is on a piece of furniture and must have a similar high gloss. There are two schools of thought on this, and all the variations between. Some sculptors like a high gloss on their work, so they sand and polish and fill and varnish or shellac, and rub down with steel wool just as furniture makers do. (There is now a plastic foam impregnated with grit, to replace steel wool.) The opposite school, of which I am a member, prefers texture, so uses sandpaper sparingly if at all, preferring to let tool marks show. Also, the wood is left without fillers or coloring, unless it be antiquing for depth, and finished with flat varnish and wax, oil and wax, or wax alone, depending upon wood and subject. We don't want a high polish, but a soft glow. There are now also several kinds of one-coat finishes, but they tend to create too high a gloss for me.

Basically, it's your choice. But test first on a scrap piece!

Index